LEAVE ME ALONE
A NOVEL OF CHENGDU

LEAVE ME ALONE
A NOVEL OF CHENGDU

MURONG

Translated by
Harvey Thomlinson

Make-Do Publishing

Make-Do Publishing
Hong Kong

Originally published in Australia by Allen & Unwin.

Copyright © Murong Xuecun 2009
Translation copyright © Harvey Thomlinson 2009

First published in 2009

Cover design Lamma Studio Design

Cover image: 'Midnight Flowers'
copyright © Oliver Rockwell 2010
www.beetabonk.com

ISBN 978-988-18419-3-3

CHAPTER ONE

My wife, Zhao Yue, called as I was leaving work. She suggested that we try this new hotpot joint in Xiyan district.

'Your life is all about food,' I said. 'Like a pig's.'

I was in a temper because Fatty Dong had just been promoted to general manager of the Sichuan branch. Fatty started at our company at the same time as me. His only talent was sucking up to people but now he was my boss and I felt depressed.

Zhao Yue said, 'If you won't come, then I'll ask someone else.'

'*Screw* someone else for all I care.'

I'd barely got that out before she ended the call.

For a while I stood in front of the phone. I knew my wife hadn't done anything wrong but I wasn't in a restrained mood. Snatching my briefcase, I stormed from the building.

Chengdu in March is all dust and smoke. I bought a pack of cigarettes at a street stand and wondered where I could spend the rest of this gloomy Friday night. After much thought, I decided to try Li Liang.

Li Liang was one of my university friends. The second year after graduation he'd quit his safe job working for a state company and started a completely new career trading futures. In less than two years he'd made a fortune of 2 or 3 million yuan. Thinking about it, I admitted that sometimes you had to believe in fate. At college no one had foreseen Li Liang's talent for investing: he'd been little more than my sidekick.

My guess was that right now if he hadn't crashed out he was playing mahjong. This was his favourite — really his only — recreation. One time at college, after thirty-seven hours of non-stop gambling during which he'd lost all his money and meal vouchers, he'd said: Chen Zhong, lend me ten yuan so I can get some food. Apparently he'd collapsed later in a small restaurant outside the campus gates.

When I arrived at Li Liang's there were three others at the table — two guys and a girl. I didn't know any of them. On seeing me, Li Liang said, 'Dude, there's beer in the fridge, DVDs in the dining room and a rubber doll in the bedroom that's never been used. Choose your pleasure!'

The others laughed.

'Screw you!' I said.

I put some money down and said, 'What are the stakes?'

The girl sitting opposite Li Liang told me double or quits. Checking my wallet, I found more than 1000 yuan, which I guessed was enough.

Li Liang introduced his guests. The two guys were from out of town and were here to learn about Li Liang's futures trading. The young woman was Ye Mei and apparently she was the daughter of the boss of some construction company. I opened a can of beer and went over to check out her tiles. Ye Mei was wearing a red sweater and a pair of tight jeans. She had full breasts and a very fine slim waist, and was jiggling her long slender legs. I felt stirrings below my waist and gulped down some beer to calm things.

After a few rounds, Li Liang got up from the table to adjust his hi-fi speakers and invited me to take his place. I immediately got mugged by Ye Mei's suite and lost 200 yuan. My luck continued to slide and a few rounds later the 1000 yuan was gone. I hit on Li Liang for some more money and he cursed and lobbed his wallet at me. At that point my mobile rang. It was Zhao Yue.

'What are you doing?' she said.

'Playing mahjong.'

'Having fun, huh?' She sounded cold.

I said it was OK, at the same time throwing out a tile.

'When are you coming home?' she asked.

'I might play all night, so don't bother waiting up for me.'

She hung up without another word.

After Zhao Yue's call, my luck turned. I kept winning big. The two guys taunted me that such good luck in gambling meant I was due for some bad luck in my private life. They joked that I should watch out my wife wasn't screwing around. Smiling, I just went on stuffing their cash into my pockets.

At 3 am, when I had cleaned up for the fourth time, Ye Mei stood and said, 'I'm out! There's something wrong here. I've never seen such disgusting good luck.'

I took an inventory of my winnings and found that I'd not only got back the lost 1000, I had an extra 3700—that was more than half my basic monthly salary. On a high, I refilled glasses for Ye Mei and myself, then leapt up on the sofa and gave an impromptu recital of one of Li Liang's poems: *Life comes all of a sudden, fuck it!*

We'd started a literature society at university—I was the president, Li Liang wrote the poetry. It was the perfect front to bed many literary college girls. As Bighead Wang from our dormitory once said: Both your hands are stained with virgins' blood.

Still, the situation at work was getting me down. I wanted to sleep but knew that I wouldn't be able to, and I'd wake up Zhao Yue if I went home. She'd ask where I'd been and we'd quarrel. The neighbours were tired of our fights, sick of the sound of smashing plates. But if I didn't go home there was nowhere to go.

I said, 'Li Liang, let's hit the road! Big brother's gonna take you for some drinks, and we'll see this babe home.'

Li Liang threw me his car keys, and said he wasn't coming. He asked me to drive the two guys to their hotel and then escort Ye Mei home. As we were leaving he warned: 'Ye Mei, take care around him, he's not a good guy. His nickname is Flower-Destroying Monk.'

Ye Mei laughed and asked if she could borrow a knife.

Li Liang said, No need. If he tries anything, just kick him in the balls.

It was deep night. As we passed the Qing Yang Palace, I suddenly remembered the first time Zhao Yue and I had gone there. With our eyes closed we'd played a game of reaching out to touch the blood-red 'longevity' character on the wall. It had turned out that I was touching the oblique 'pie' stroke and she was touching the stubby 'dot'.

I'd said, You can enjoy your longevity since you got the 'cock'.[2]

Zhao Yue had laughed her head off. Right now she would be asleep, and I imagined her cuddling a pillow, snoring, with the light on. Coming home after a business trip once, I'd found her just like that.

Ye Mei lit a cigarette and said, 'Are you thinking about your mistress? You have an evil smile.'

I said, 'Yeah, I'm thinking of you. When we get these

two back to the hotel, you come home with me, OK?'

'Unfortunately, I couldn't take your wife's slapping.'

I smiled, and thought nastily that it was OK as long as she could take me.

I've never been able to resist sexual temptation. Li Liang even wrote a poem about me:

> *Tonight the sunlight is bright and beautiful*
> *Dancing with hormones*
> *Chengdu, your soft skin*
> *Is like my sad mood*
> *Walking naked in God's smile*
> *I couldn't choose at Yanshikou in March*

Couldn't choose actually meant *unwilling to choose*. Li Liang had laid into me once, saying I wouldn't let even a pig get away. To make his point he checked off my girlfriends on his fingers:

- That PE teacher with bad skin.
- The 150-kilo restaurant boss.
- The waitress who was ugly enough to frighten you.
- And that fried breadstick sales girl who ate garlic.

I responded that he simply didn't appreciate women. For example:

- The PE teacher was tall, 177 centimetres, and her nickname was 'dark rose'.

- The restaurant boss was as plump as the famous Imperial concubine Yang.[3]
- That waitress was hot. Her chest size was 36F, so she looked as if she was going to topple over when walking. If she did, her breasts would hit the ground before her face did.
- And don't you think my breadstick lover looked like that hottie Ning Dongdong in our class?

Li Liang just muttered, Dude, you're not picky at all.

After dropping off the two guys, Ye Mei and I were alone. I deliberately drove slowly, staring at her until she seemed uncomfortable. Her face reddened. When I smirked, she lost it.

'What's so funny?'

I asked if she was a virgin or not.

She glared. 'Too bad I didn't borrow that knife from Li Liang so I could chop it off.'

In my experience, if a girl was willing to banter with you in this way it meant she didn't mind being seduced. Also, I'd read somewhere that women's resistance was at its weakest after midnight. Stopping the car with the excuse of adjusting the rearview mirror, I pressed against her. She trembled slightly but didn't move away, and so I slid my arm around her slender waist.

She protested. 'You are bad. If you try that again, I'll have to get out of the car.'

I sighed and reluctantly withdrew my arm.

Then she murmured, 'Who gave you the right to win all my money anyway?'

Hearing this I was elated and held her tight.

CHAPTER TWO

The Chengdu I knew was like an chaotic courtyard inhabited by hundreds of different families. In junior high days I lived on Jinsi Street, just a hundred metres away from the incense of fragrant, flourishing Wenshu Temple. I used to go there with my parents to burn joss sticks and chat over tea with friends and strangers alike. Whole afternoons would pass this way. Now my parents were old and I'd grown up. Life in Chengdu was so dull that novels and TV dramas seemed completely fantastic.

After seeing Ye Mei home, I was knackered. There was something cold and wet on my underwear—clearly I hadn't cleaned up properly after I'd finished. What was worse, Ye Mei had appeared dissatisfied with my performance. She acted cold when she got out of the car and it upset me. I drove to the underground parking lot at

Vancouver Square, put down the car seat and crashed out right there.

When I woke up my back was murder. I looked at the clock: nearly eleven. Some guy knocked at my window and asked if I had any spare gas. I opened the trunk, took out a small gas can and said he was welcome to it. This was a company product, and there were at least a dozen cans in Li Liang's Audi A6. Our boss was from a decayed family of once-high officials. Due to the former status of his ancestors, he enjoyed connections with large state-owned enterprises to which he sold car parts and gas. He'd also opened car repair shops in several cities. Business was hot, and in barely ten years he'd made several million. After handing over the gas, I got depressed again thinking about my job. Over the last few years I had contributed a good 100 million in sales, and 20 million net profits, to the company. Fatty Dong had done nothing but fart, but he'd managed to become my boss.

Today, Chengdu was blazing with sunlight. Like most creatures of the night, I avoided the sun. A recent article in the *Sichuan Legal Newspaper* had said 'dark things can never bear the light'. Secretly I admitted that I was well on my way to becoming a part of the dark side. How, when just a couple of years ago, I had been an enthusiastic youth, a purposeful university student?

A sad song by Mavis Hee came out of the car speakers:

Legend has it that tears can shatter the city
Red eyes looking sadly at the lonely city

Fireworks fade
Songs stop

It made me think of Zhao Yue. Suddenly I was guilty, and I went to the People's Department Store and bought her a wonderbra that cost over 700 yuan. Zhao Yue had said that she didn't get much exercise these days and her breasts were perhaps getting a bit saggy. I realised I didn't take good care of her. When I looked at the clothes I was wearing, all designer stuff bought by her, I felt bad about my adventures last night.

When I got home Zhao Yue was sat on the couch watching TV. She acted as if she hadn't seen me. Throwing down the bra, I went into the bathroom and took a cold shower. Afterwards I found her in bed, facing the wall. When I hugged her, I didn't get any response, and so I drifted off to sleep.

Muddled with a dream I heard her muttering on the phone.

'My husband is home now so I can't talk. Call me some other time.'

Opening my eyes, I asked, 'You got a lover now?'

She nodded.

'Good work,' I said. 'You're really doing well.'

She smiled, and nodded. 'People always want to better themselves.'

'What does the guy do?' I asked.

'He's an entrepreneur.'

I sat up. 'Let's make a deal. When you've cheated him out of his money, give me half.'

Zhao Yue said she wasn't kidding.

'I know, I know,' I said. 'The foreign policy of our family is "developing external relations" and "bringing in foreign currency".'[4]

Zhao Yue is someone else I met at university. She was in the year below me, one of the three most beautiful girls in the class of '92. Our campus often had a problem with hooligans from the town breaking in, and one time a gang caught Zhao Yue and her former boyfriend making out in the woods. Her boyfriend ran away before he'd even pulled up his trousers. It was said that when he got to the dorm the condom fell out of the leg of his pants. Zhao Yue was just about to shut her eyes and give in to her attackers when Bighead Wang and I stumbled across them on our way home after a heavy drinking session. We fought those thugs to protect Zhao Yue's name. My belief was that any man's fantasies of heroism would have been aroused seeing Zhao Yue wearing just a shirt with her panties round her knees. Bighead speculated afterwards that Zhao Yue and her boyfriend were expert at doing it from behind. The slang for this was 'getting fire from the mountains'. If Zhao Yue wasn't my wife, I'd be more than happy to dwell on this image. Conversely, if I'd known that Zhao Yue would become my wife, I doubt whether I'd have been such a hero. Li Liang said that I was too fond of perverse logic, and he was referring to my love life. Even now, Zhao Yue tried to avoid Bighead.

I didn't really think Zhao Yue was easy. She'd only had a couple of boyfriends on campus. Actually, on getting to know her she'd turned out to be quite refined. She was gentle, sweet and loyal to me. But whenever I thought about the scene that day, I felt depressed. Life: you just needed to know the basic information, just see a few things clearly. You didn't need to look into all the particulars otherwise it became boring and meaningless. There was plenty of evidence for this. For example, Fatty Dong had a friend who'd opened a wife-swapping club. Everyone there fucked other people's spouses and saw their own spouses being fucked by others. Legend had it that ninety per cent of couples divorced straight after leaving the club.

But Zhao Yue wasn't candid. She'd always maintained that the incident in the woods was her first time, and insisted that it hadn't entered fully. When you're showing a person tolerance and they won't admit the truth, it's frustrating. In response I'd decided on the following strategy: to sympathise, educate, and then help Zhao Yue to understand the seriousness of the issue.

No matter if it's the first time, or the hundredth time, it's the same thing, I told her. You know I don't care about numbers. Whether it enters completely or just halfway, it's still sex.

Sociologists have researched everything but the psychology of a husband being willingly betrayed. I often wondered whether my many affairs came from a subconscious desire for revenge. But there was nothing to take revenge for. I'd had several women before Zhao Yue. That PE teacher was one of them. Even after I fell in love with Zhao Yue, the teacher and I once romped on a weights machine after a PE class.

I didn't take seriously Zhao Yue's claim that she had a lover. Women always try to get attention by playing mind games, and so I wasn't interested in her imaginary entrepreneur. Zhao Yue often said she would introduce him to me. I said if she dared I would give him a good thrashing.

CHAPTER THREE

After our general manager was fired, Head Office sent in a team to do an audit. At the same time they carried out a bit of 'propaganda work'. They called us to a meeting—more than two hundred people stuffed into a room almost full to bursting. A young court eunuch droned on for ages. He urged us to be loyal to the company, to give more and demand less, to work but not complain. He even trotted out a saying from the classics: *Persistent in work; indifferent towards profit.*

I thought, motherfucker, we're all wage-slaves; is there any need to dress it up like this? Then I heard him mention my name.

'Manager Chen is the backbone of the Sichuan branch,' he said. 'In the last few years he has made a big contribution. He's not afraid to take responsibility. All we need is for everyone to follow Manager Chen's lead and our company will achieve great things.'

I felt sick. This had to be Fatty Dong's trickery.

That dickhead had naturally rushed to sit at the front with the eunuch from head office. He looked like a well-behaved grandson, his notebook spread on his knee, his neck straight. His fat face was one big smile. When the time came to make his own report, he gave me another subtle kick in passing: 'Manager Chen, you have great abilities, but you're not such a good team-player."

I looked at him. The phony was wearing an elegant pair of trousers with braces, and was bent over the desk writing something in his notebook. I cursed him silently: Fuck you. Are your farts really worth writing down?

After the meeting was over, Fatty Dong dragged me to his office and set to work on me. He said that he'd never expected to be appointed company leader and had protested several times that he wasn't worthy. Apparently he'd recommended me to be general manager, but the company had said that although I had ability, I wasn't ready. 'You still need to gain more experience,' he told me importantly.

Crap, I thought. You're making all this up.

When Fatty had finished his spiel, he pretended to be friends. 'I know you,' he said. 'You hadn't even thought about the general manager position.'

'That's way beyond someone ignorant like me, who can't shut up,' I responded. 'What I need, Boss Dong, is for someone as mature and experienced as you to guide me.'

Fatty Dong smiled magnificently, and I seized the

opportunity to ambush him.

'Could you see whether it's possible to raise my salary? I'm saving for a house and money is tight. Also, our sales department always exceeds its targets, so I don't see why we should get less than office staff.'

His fat smile melted like an ice-cream on the beach.

I called the sales team together for a meeting and punched the air aggresively.

'Brothers, good news! I've already applied to get everyone a raise. Screw you, Liu Three, if you're handing round the cigarettes, give me one!'

Liu Three laughed and tossed me a Red Pagoda cigarette, then Zhou Weidong bent his head and lit it for me.

'Fatty Dong opposed the increase,' I explained. 'He made me beg three times before he finally agreed to fight for this with Head Office. Let's all watch Boss Dong carefully.'

I deliberately gave those two words 'Boss Dong' a mean bite. Secretly I was thinking: Fatty Dong, there's no way I can get this gang of more than a hundred people to like you. Getting them to hate you though would be just too easy.

For so many people to get a salary increase at the same time would mean at least a twenty per cent increase in the Sichuan branch's budget. If Fatty dared to make this request to Head Office and didn't get rebuked then I'd be his bitch. But if he didn't make the request then how could he manage the sales department?

The meeting room was thick with smoke. The news of a possible raise put everyone on a high. The steam repair department chief, Zhou Yan, one of the few women in the company, called out, Big brother, if they really increase our salaries we'll all throw in some money to get you a mistress.

Liu Three said, 'If you're thinking about getting Big Brother a mistress, then just come out and say so, no need to be coy. It can be arranged. He grinned at me. What's more, Zhou Yan has big breasts.'

The group of flunkies all laughed. Zhou Yan gave me a look, her face as red as paint. Actually I'd sensed early on that she had some kind of crush on me, but according to traditional values a rabbit doesn't eat the grass near its own burrow. How could I have the balls to give someone instructions by day and then at night stretch out my hand to take off her skirt?

During lunch my university friend Bighead Wang gave me a call. He asked whether my company could do some government car plates. I said that it might be possible, but it all depended who they were for.

'Just do them,' Bighead said. 'It's me that wants them.'

'OK, let's call Li Liang and go to Old Mother's Hotpot restaurant for a few beers,' I said. 'We can talk about it then.'

After graduation, Bighead Wang had joined the police bureau. On reporting for duty, he'd insisted that he didn't want a desk job, he wanted to be on the beat. Li Liang and I both called him a stupid dickhead. On the contrary, he replied, we were the dickheads, and then he revealed his 'rights' theory.

'Cops on the beat are allowed to be corrupt, but pen-pushers can only wag their tails obediently,' he told us. He went on: 'An inside section chief can get around 1000 yuan a month, whereas I hear that a cop on the beat can get several thousand. You tell me which type of public servant is more important?'

This decision demonstrated Bighead's genius. Five years later he was already the head of a busy downtown precinct. He had a car and a house, and he was about twenty kilos fatter than at the time of graduation. I often told him that if he were a pig, twenty kilos would be enough to feed a family for a whole month.

After work I drove the company's Santana to Old Mother's Hotpot restaurant in the heart of downtown. There I found Bighead already established in a booth and hitting on a young hostess. Bighead fancied himself as the literary type. He'd collected loads of books, mostly European and American. He bragged that he never forgot anything he read, and was always ready to give people his take on Duras' *The Lovers*, as well as Jules Verne's *Twenty Thousand Leagues Under the Sea*. When I arrived, the guy was quoting from the classics: *Husband and wife were two birds in a forest, but when disaster came they both flew off. While you're alive she'll be loving, but when you're dead she'll leave with the others.*

I had some tea and then said, 'It works better as *While you're alive she'll screw you every day, when you die she'll screw other people.*'

The young girl made a hasty retreat. I said to Bighead, 'Yet again you're scheming to ruin a girl from a good family.'

Bighead patted his belly and told me that he'd seen Zhao Yue going off with this stud, looking very furtive. 'Now you're green with envy,' he said.

When we rescued Zhao Yue from the gang in the woods, Bighead Wang and I made an agreement that we wouldn't tell anyone what had happened. A few days later, Zhao Yue treated us to a meal. When she showed up she was dressed plainly, without make-up. The whole time she kept her head lowered and hardly spoke.

'You're being very quiet,' I said to her. 'We can't enjoy our drinking.'

Zhao Yue, her eyes brimming with tears, just wanted to say one thing: 'I won't forget your kindness, but if anyone finds out what happened, I will have to kill myself immediately.'

Bighead Wang and I swore that if we ever talked about this we were total bastards. On the road back to the dormitory, Bighead said something that moved me: 'Zhao Yue really is a sad creature.'

'Too right,' I agreed, and thinking about her tear-filled eyes I felt a little pained.

Li Liang pushed open the restaurant door. As he came in

he was gesticulating while yelling into his phone, 'Quick, buy as many as you can.'

Today he was wearing a neatly pressed business suit and his glossy hair was in a centre part.

Bighead said quietly, 'The son of a bitch looks like a duck.'

Li Liang told us he didn't have any choice, it was to impress his mother-in-law. That afternoon he'd gone to his girlfriend's family's place. They were getting married on 1 May.

Surprised, I asked him which family's daughter had been so unlucky as to fall into his evil hands.

He said, 'You know her. Ye Mei.'

My heart skipped a beat as I said, 'Fuck me.'

I wondered whether or not I should tell him what had happened that night I'd driven Ye Mei home.

After toasting Li Liang with spirits we called for beers. Li Liang's expression was very happy. He said that he planned to buy a villa by the banks of the Funan River. 'We'll live upstairs, and downstairs will be our mahjong parlour and games room.'

I said, 'After you get married will you go to the wife-swapping club?'

He shook his head, looking slightly embarrassed, but then said, 'If you bring Zhao Yue along, I'll swap with you.'

I'd once told Li Liang about the club that belonged to Fatty's friend. It was called the Same Music Private Members Club. At the time, Li Liang had groaned in admiration. His mouth watering, he'd said that if he had a wife he would definitely take her there to broaden her knowledge. Later, Fatty Dong had warned me that his friend had links with both cops and gangs so we'd better stay away from the club.

When I mentioned this place, Bighead was all agog. He demanded to know *what* wife-swapping club: 'How come I've never heard of it?' I gave him a vivid description, and his eyes widened. Sucking in a deep breath, he finally sighed and said, 'The world has such wonders!'

Ye Mei called while we were eating. Li Liang was nauseating: he sat in a corner cooing while all the time continuing to put the beers away. After a while he said that Ye Mei wanted to talk to me for a minute. It was noisy in the bar—Bighead was picking his teeth and watching football and refused to turn the TV down—so I had to go out to the passageway.

I heard Ye Mei say something like, 'I didn't come.'

I said, 'Who didn't come?'

'It isn't who, it's *that*.'

'Come on, what the hell are you talking about?'

Ye Mei was suddenly furious. 'Fuck you. I mean my period didn't come.'

'Couldn't this be Li Liang's disaster?' I said eventually.

Ye Mei cursed me again, claiming that she'd never even touched Li Liang's hand. I was angry too. No one had sworn at me like that for a long time.

I said coldly, 'So what are you going to do?'

She suddenly started crying. 'If I knew what to do, why would I be talking to you?'

My brain made calculations at lightning speed. I realised this couldn't be resolved in Chengdu and so I said, 'On Saturday we'll go to Leshan for the abortion. Think of something to tell Li Liang.'

CHAPTER FOUR

On the streets of Chengdu every face can seem familiar, each look can contain a deeper meaning. A flash of the eyes, a casual turn of the head, can make the gates of memory burst open and the past flood out. Once, when I was buying cigarettes outside the entrance to Du Fu's cottage,[5] the old cigarette-vendor addressed me by my childhood name: 'Rabbit, you've grown so big.'

She said that years ago she'd been my neighbour, but although I racked my brain I couldn't remember ever having a neighbour like her.

Then there was the time I crawled drunk into a three-wheeled cab and the driver said, 'You're doing pretty well for yourself.'

I said, 'Who the fuck are you? I don't know you.'

'I'm your primary school classmate Chen Three! We

stole a girl's bag together once. Have you completely forgotten?'

I thought there had to be something seriously wrong with my memory. From a certain point in time, the record of my life was being erased section by section. Whose bag had I stolen? Who had I walked with hand in hand by the banks of the Funan River? Whose smile had driven me crazy all that time ago?

I can't remember.

Then what do you remember?

Many events of my colourful past were now vague, blurred like birds flying by. I could see myself in countless drinking establishments holding up a glass. I could picture the smiles of people I'd once known. I could see girls of every shape and size lying with me, waiting for dawn in the curve of my arm. There were a few details that were still vivid—the me of 1998 in a smart suit sitting in the Diamond Entertainment City with my arms around a gaudily made-up hostess, getting her to guess how many of my fingers were reaching inside her skirt.

'Three,' she'd said.

'Wrong!' Making a fanfare, I'd lifted her skirt. 'It's four.'

Fatty Dong banged on my office door. Since becoming general manager, Fatty was an even more magnificent sight, walking around very proudly just as a top official should.

I said, 'Boss Dong your graciousness, what words of

wisdom do you have for me?'

'You little prick. I'll tell you some good news: Head Office has approved a raise for the sales team, but it can't be everyone. At most, twenty per cent. Make a list of who should get the raise and have it on my desk by tomorrow.'

I cursed as I watched his ungainly behind retreating. Fatty might look like a pig but I'd underestimated his IQ. Now it didn't matter to whom I gave a raise, the rest of them would naturally resent me. If Fatty Dong wanted to stir things up even more, he could put it about that those who got the increase were my cronies, while those who didn't were my enemies. The trust that I'd painstakingly established in the sales team would be destroyed.

Spreading rumours was Fatty Dong's specialty. Our former general manager had been forced out as a result of one of Fatty's letters. The letter alleged that our former manager had committed several offenses such as carrying on with female staff, accepting bribes, and spending company money extravagantly. No way was I going to let Fatty get me as well.

I called the sales managers of the steam repair unit, the fittings unit and the oil materials unit to my office. I assigned the quota of names for the raise between them and I told each of them to submit me a list separately.

Zhou Yan said, 'Big Brother, forget about the mistress idea. It seems there's only enough cash for a one-night stand.'

Liu Three gave me a malicious wink. I didn't respond, just smiled and watched Zhou Yan leave the room. Large, ripe buttocks and two long and slender legs, with skin like snow.

When I got home, I told Zhao Yue that I wanted 5000 yuan.

What do you need it for? she asked.

I said that I'd been careless and got a girl from a good family pregnant and she had to have an abortion. This was part of my skill in handling Zhao Yue: each time I told her the truth, she thought I was winding her up. The more I tried to cover things up, the more desperate she was to know what was really going on. Many of the bowls in our house have got smashed that way.

Zhao Yue said ferociously, 'If you ever dare to mess up like that, I'll cut it off.'

When I held her tightly to my chest, she became a soft ball of flesh. I sighed and thought that Zhao Yue really had no idea.

'Why do you really need the money?' she asked.

'At the weekend I have to go to Leshan on business.'

'Why don't you borrow from the company?'

'I haven't repaid the money I borrowed last time,' I told her. 'If you have debts then you can't borrow any more.'

As I spoke I felt a twinge of anxiety, reflecting that in the past few years I'd run up a debt to the company of something like 200,000 yuan. Somehow I had to think of a way to set things right. When that eunuch had come to do the audit, he'd spent ages grilling me about the debt issue.

On top of that, Ye Mei's pregnancy had me nervous like

never before. In the past I'd got a few girls knocked up — for example, my breadstick lover, as well as a Sichuan University English department student. However, they weren't any problem. I just gave them a few thousand yuan and everything was sweet, they were content to sort it out themselves. They didn't need me to go with them. But this time, unexpectedly, it was my best friend's fiancé and so I felt bad.

Saturday lunchtime I drove to meet Ye Mei at Jinxiu Gardens. Her cheeks were red with blusher. She was wearing a pink sleeveless tight-fitting top over her firm, high chest. I asked her what she'd told Li Liang and she told me resentfully to mind my own business.

I stuck a Richard Clayderman CD in the player. All the way to Leshan we didn't say a word to each other.

Whenever I go to Leshan I stay at the Jiuyuefeng Hotel. The scenery there is beautiful; you only have to walk a few steps to come to the Leshan Giant Buddha.[6] The best thing though is that many of Leshan's most beautiful girls are gathered in this area. In 1996, when the hotel sauna had just opened, a local client took me there whoring. More than one hundred babes with stunning figures lined up for us to choose from. The client said, 'Young Chen, have you ever been an emperor?' I said, 'What do you mean, an emperor?' He said, 'Two girls.' My mouth started to water. I said, 'I want to be an emperor.' That day we spent at least 5000 yuan. At the end of it I thought that being an emperor was a fine thing.

Ye Mei and I took separate rooms. I said, 'Today you should rest; tomorrow I'll go with you to the hospital.' After a two-hour car journey she seemed tired. Thinking back to that fateful night, I wondered what Ye Mei had been thinking when I took off her clothes. Zhao Yue would have been long asleep while all that was going on. What had she been dreaming of?

When my mind turned to Zhao Yue, I became upset. For many years, I'd seldom given her a thought whenever I'd been away from home continuing my life of debauchery. Zhao Yue also often went to care for my parents. In fact, evidence suggested that my mother and father were closer to her than they were to me. At Spring Festival last year they'd presented us with a written dedication for our new home which had read: *Unfilial son, filial daughter.* Zhao Yue's salary was quite low but she'd stumped up most of the deposit for our apartment. The day before when I got home, she'd been eating a pack of cheap instant noodles. My heart had suddenly ached. After more than five years, I thought, I'd played around enough. It was time to sort myself out, live respectably. Love my wife well.

At that very moment it began to rain. The river water billowed, the leaves shook on the trees. I saw lightning split the sky and vowed, This time when I get back to Chengdu, I'll settle my debt to the company and try my best to lead a decent life.

Ye Mei went out to get something to eat. I stayed in the room smoking cigarettes,and slagging off the first half of my life. When Ye Mei got back, after she shoved open the door, she took one of my cigarettes and lit it. She then gave me a piercing look. When I asked her what was up she didn't just carried on staring straight at me. I felt nervous and said, 'Are you suffering from a nervous disorder?'

Ye Mei lay on her back, sprawled across the bed. 'Fuck you,' she said, and took another drag of her cigarette. 'Come and play with me one more time.'

I didn't know whether to laugh or cry. I said, 'First, it's not nice to curse people. Secondly, you're my best friend's fiancée now, so there's no way I can screw you again.'

Ye Mei said, 'Fuck, have you started to be a good boy? Don't you remember how forceful you were that day?'

She sprang up suddenly and threw me onto the bed. She was really quite strong.

CHAPTER FIVE

Li Liang decided he would throw his wedding party at the Minshan Hotel. He asked me to arrange the banquet and the cars. When I wanted to know on what scale the event would be, he started bragging.

'Fifty tables, each table 2000 yuan. At least twenty cars, nothing lower than a Lexus.'

'Such a big spender,' I said. 'Have you got money to burn?'

He laughed. 'In this life I plan to get married only once, so I have to have a big wedding to make everyone jealous.'

Li Liang generally chose his words very carefully, so this comment wasn't necessarily throw-away vulgarity.

Once again I couldn't help wondering whether he knew what had happened between Ye Mei and me. The day of the abortion he'd called me for some reason. When I asked him where he was he said he was walking outside with Ye Mei. Like an idiot I almost blurted out that he was lying. I was thinking, you big fibber, Ye Mei is on the operating table right now. Li Liang had giggled, then hung up sounding evasive.

After the abortion, I'd told Ye Mei about this and she said, 'Li Liang is weird, but you're just a stupid ass.'

That evening Ye Mei had been unbridled and crazy, making me feel as though I was being raped. Strong wind and rain buffeted the window. Ye Mei's wild hair was all across my body while her hands tore roughly at my own hair.

'How about being gentle?' I asked.

She gnashed her teeth and snarled, 'Screw you, no way.'

I'd never imagined the body of this girl could contain such power. She was like a female wolf whose cub has been killed, snapping at my body a bite at a time. It scared the fuck out of me.

As she came, Ye Mei fell prostrate on top of me and cried. Her hair was soft and her skin was slippery. Her tears dripped one at a time onto my face; cold, bitter and astringent, making me remember many things past. I was full of guilt and pity, and a kind of inexpressible tenderness. I lay there until she'd pressed all the air out of me, then I patted her arse and told her to get up. Ye Mei got up obediently from the bed, dressed herself and gave the mirror a silent, beautiful smile. Then she pushed open the door and left without saying a word.

On the road back to Chengdu I stopped the car and bought Ye Mei a pair of farm chickens. I told her that she should feed them well. She seemed moved. Recently, I thought I'd changed a little and learned how to be considerate, perhaps because I was getting older. While music played on the car stereo, Ye Mei slept deeply like a child.

It was already after six when I got back. I said to Zhao Yue, 'What's the name of that hotpot place you wanted to try? Let's go together this evening.'

Zhao Ye looked surprised. 'Don't you need to entertain clients tonight?'

'I don't want to entertain anyone,' I said. 'Tonight I want to devote myself to my wife.'

She laughed. 'Too bad that I have to go out to a dinner party.' And, snatching her leather bag she clattered off down the stairs in her black high-heels.

Home alone, I became increasingly bored, unbearably depressed. I had this irritated feeling that I wasn't being taken seriously. Soon I'd got through two bottles of beer and almost worn out the TV remote control. Slightly unhinged, I gave Zhao Yue a call and demanded to know what time she'd be back.

'Don't wait up,' she said, 'I want to stay a bit longer.'

Hearing this I felt angry. I pulled out my mobile phone and called Li Liang to ask him to come to Dong Dong disco with me.

'You loser, don't you have anything better to do?' he said. Then I heard him saying to someone else: 'Son of a bitch wants to go to Dong Dong disco.'

Of course, he had to be talking to Ye Mei.

Dong Dong disco is one of Chengdu's most famous places. Originally it was a civil air defence shelter. After the city opened up to the outside world, one part of it became an underground market, while another part housed a number of hostess bars. They claimed to be discos but I'd never actually seen people dancing there. Men went there to hold a girl in their arms and touch her everywhere while having evil thoughts. At the end of a song they'd hand over a 10 yuan tip and consider the transaction over.

I'd just walked into the disco when this tall girl I'd encountered before came up to me. She said that she hadn't seen me for a long time. I patted her butt and said I wasn't dancing today, just looking. She turned and embraced some fat guy instead. The two seemed to be stuck to each other like glue. The girl swayed as she rubbed her hips rhythmically against Fatty's crotch. Fatty slobbered and his two pig's trotters went groping up and down her body. The girl smiled at me with an 'I can't do anything about it' look. Suddenly I remembered that she had a huge black mole on her back. It was definitely enough to scare a man into losing his libido.

At that moment all the lights went out. The disco was full of ghostly shadows. My eyes couldn't get used to it and I staggered around until someone gently pulled at my clothes, asking me to sit down. I sat, and in the shadows a face gradually appeared before me. My breadstick lover was smiling at me.

After Li Liang's graduation he lived at my house for a

fortnight, then rented his own place in Luoguo Alley. By then I was depressed at home and so I moved in with him. At the mouth of the alley was a snack restaurant. It was there that I first encountered my breadstick lover. She had only recently moved from her village. She wore old, faded clothes, and even in July she kept her buttons tightly fastened as she toiled over the fried breadsticks in their seething pots.

'Aren't you hot?' I asked her.

Her face turned red. It made me think of a girl on our class's study committee, Ning Dong Dong ... The night before graduation, Ning Dong Dong and I enjoyed a long kiss behind the rockery. As I quietly unfastened her bra, Ning Dong Dong moaned. Just as I was ready to progress to third base however, she regained her senses, said 'I can't' three times and ran away to her dormitory. This was my third greatest regret of my university career. As for the others—one was failing the fourth-level examination three times (the most unlucky time being short half a point); another was getting busted the time I rented a screening room to show porn movies. My dreams of riches were shattered.

It appeared that my breadstick lover was interested in me from the very beginning. The breadsticks she chose for me were always large and juicy, which made Li Liang very jealous. Behind Li Liang's back, I went to flirt with her a few times. She usually laughed at my teasing, but didn't give in to it either, which fascinated me. Then the day came when she asked whether I could help her find a place to live. I was wild with joy and told her that could be arranged. On the day she moved into my house, I had my way with her. She didn't call out or shout, just struggled incessantly, grabbing at me so my whole body was mauled. After I'd finished, I was suddenly afraid and said dejectedly, 'You should report this.'

She didn't reply, but after a while took my hand and said, 'Let's do it again, but be gentle this time.'

After that my breadstick lover lived with me for three months. Every day she would wash my clothes, make food, and tidy and clean the room. When she saw me walk in the door, her face would light up. That period of time is vividly clear in my memory. Day after day I would go to work, go home, watch TV and make love. Later, I thought it was probably the closest I'd come to real happiness in my whole life. Once, because she'd eaten a clove of garlic, I cursed her and made her cry. That was the strongest memory I had from that time.

When Zhao Yue was ready to come to Chengdu, I told my breadstick lover, 'My girlfriend is coming. We have to split up.'

She froze with terror. Tears flowed down her face.

'It's no good being like this,' I told her.

She didn't say a word, just cried soundlessly all night. I couldn't get her to stop and it made me very sad. When the sky was nearly light she wiped her tears away, kissed my face and said, 'Chen Zhong, give me a little money. I need to have an abortion.'

I admit that I'm not a responsible guy; I was just

interested in her body. After we split up she called me a few times. Because I was afraid Zhao Yue would start to wonder, whenever I heard it was her I just hung up. I'd never imagined I'd meet her again one day in a place like this.

'Do you want to dance?' she said. 'I won't ask you for money.'

My heart suddenly flooded with sorrow. All around I saw men and women pressed tightly together, using every revolting posture you could think of to rub against each other. Turning my head, I looked at this once so simple girl. What did she feel when these men groped her? Did she think of me?

'Why are you here?' I asked.

She lowered her head. 'For money. Do you really need to ask?'

'Don't you want to go home?'

On the day we split up, I'd asked her what she would do in the future. She said that she would go back to her village and never leave again.

The disco was filling up with more and more people. A few men reached out for her, but she rejected them. Leaning against my shoulder, she sighed and said, 'I don't want to go back to the village. I can't take the suffering. It's hard to be a peasant now.'

Her hand felt unfamiliarly soft and smooth. I remembered that when I first knew my breadstick lover her hands were still hard, rough to the touch. What was it that had made this simple unaffected young woman become a dancing girl, maybe even a prostitute? In that gloomy, dirty disco,

I thought, was it me? Was it the city? Or was it just life?

When the disco hall began to empty, I got out 1000 yuan. She refused emotionly. I said, 'OK, let me see you home.'

She laughed. 'No need. I live with my boyfriend so it's not that convenient.'

I asked her what her boyfriend did.

'He works on a construction site.'

After a pause, she seemed to read the question in my heart. 'He knows where I am.'

I opened the taxi door, and then heard her call my name. I turned my head to see a glimmer of tears in her eyes. She said brokenly, 'If you ever think of me, text me. OK?'

CHAPTER SIX

In our regular Monday morning meeting, Fatty Dong went on and on about 'professionalism'. 'Dress professionally, speak professionally, adopt a professional mentality,' he said. As he worked himself into a frenzy he almost seemed to dance; his feet skipped, his lardy body trembled.

I was sat beside him smoking and wondering why as soon as someone was made an official they became so hypocritical. Last July, Fatty and I had entertained some clients. In the nightclub we'd chosen a few girls. His expression had been terrifying, and then I suddenly understood the true meaning of the word 'ravage'. If I hadn't been with him, he'd likely have devoured his girl. She started off smiling but soon was trying to evade him, then pushed him away. Finally she gave this terrifying cry. As well as his own girl, he also molested mine, asking everyone whether her breasts were genuine or fake. What colour underwear was she wearing? Of course, he had to inspect. When his girl finally asked for her tip, the jerk called her to the door and haggled over the price.

'You're not just doing this for the money,' he told her. 'We were getting on well together.'

A moment later, we heard him say righteously, 'How can you be like this? You're depraved! Here's 100 yuan, do you want it or not? Hey, get your hands off my wallet!'

At this point, our client, Zhou Dajiang, finally stepped in. Taking out a pile of notes, he said, 'Miss is hard-working. Give back the 100 yuan. Please accept this money.'

Fatty Dong didn't see this intervention as shameful. He saw it as an honour. The next day he told me proudly, 'When you go out to play it's best to spend as little money as you can and scrounge off others as much as possible. Chen Zhong, if you learn from me you'll be OK.'

I replied, 'You are too wise for me.' What I was really thinking was: some people are admirable and others obscene, but then there's you.'

The day after our visit to the club Zhou Dajiang gave me a call and really laid into Fatty Dong: 'Fuck him, I've never seen such scum.'

Zhou Dajiang is a north-easterner and his manner is very frank and open.

At the Monday meeting, once Fatty Dong had finished blustering, he waved his hand just like a great leader and asked me, 'Manager Chen, is there anything you would like to say?'

I thought, yes, I'll say a few words and show you what real talent is.

I stood up and cleared my throat, then said that Boss Dong's suggestions were deserving of praise.

'The question of professionalism is basically about how to discharge one's obligations,' I continued. 'Professional dress and professional language are external, but the most important thing is your achievements. If you can't meet your targets (here I looked meaningfully at the sales team) it doesn't matter if you wear smart suits every day and make some bullshit excuses. You're still an idiot.'

When I turned back to Fatty Dong, I saw that his face had turned as purple as a rotten eggplant.

At the end of the day, the accountant came looking for me. He said there was a problem with the expenses form I'd submitted the previous week for a large promotion with some petrol stations. Because there was no confirmation letter from the stations, they were unable to pay up.

This promotion was one I'd arranged jointly with Sichuan petrol companies: if you spent more than 500 yuan at one of their outlets, your car could get a free check-up at one of our repair centres. The check-up was paid for by the petrol stations. In one month we'd made more than 200,000 from repair work alone. You could say that it was decent business. The expenses form I'd put in was for 18,000 yuan, around 3,000 of which was padding. You see, just like a song I once heard in a bar: *My effort is large, my reward is small, every day I struggle for a small profit, buying and selling.*

The world is unfair. Only a small part of the money made from your talent comes to you. Most of it goes to that boss you hardly ever see. So I often dredged for a few perks from my business. I believed that moral behaviour was only possible when one had no anxiety about clothing or feeding oneself. For example, if Li Liang were to do my job there was no way he'd be as devious as me.

Glaring at the accountant, I explained that the petrol stations all belonged to the Sichuan People's Petrol Company. Who was I supposed to get to confirm my expenses?

The accountant smiled sympathetically and said this was Fatty Dong's initiative. 'You should discuss it with Boss Dong.'

I flung open the door to Fatty Dong's office and slapped the expense report down on the table.

'Boss Dong, what the hell is this about?' I demanded. 'Are you going to let people do their job or not?'

Fatty Dong spoke like an official. 'Chen Zhong, don't get agitated. I've done everything by the company regulations.'

'Please be clear,' I said. 'Just say whether or not you want to do this promotion. If you don't want to do it any more, I'll call up the Sichuan Petrol Company.'

Fatty Dong hesitated, then angrily signed the expenses form.

After I'd got the money from accounts I called Zhao Yue and told her I'd treat her to dinner at the Jinjiang Hotel. She sounded less than enthusiastic, saying there was no need to be so extravagant. Zhao Yue was always very frugal. If we spent more than 100 yuan she felt bad. Once I splashed out 700 yuan on some perfume for her, but she was reluctant to wear it. When I was in a good mood I'd tease her: 'You belong to the white-collar class, so how come you're like a little match girl?'

She usually laughed and said, 'Me, white collar? At most I'm the dependant of a white-collar worker.'

After work I went to the flower shop downstairs and bought a 268 yuan bunch of red roses. The salesgirl grinned widely. On the card I wrote: *Wife, if you fatten up a bit you would be even better looking, so eat up!*

The girl gave me an even more simpering smile.

I said, 'Am I good to my wife?'

'It's touching,' she said. 'In the future, if I look for a husband I will look for one like you.'

Her words made me feel empty.

With the flowers I cut a dashing figure as I walked into the Jinjiang Hotel. People stared at me. I chose a two-person table just near the window, then sent Zhao Yue a text: *Husband's already here, come and eat.*

This was our secret sex language. There were many ways for us to 'eat': missionary, cowgirl, doggy. Sadly though, Zhao Yue would never 'eat' with her mouth. I imagined her naughty smile when she saw the message, and felt myself swell with lust. Zhou Dajiang had given me two Viagra pills and I wondered whether tonight might be the time to try them.

You get great service in five-star hotels. In less than one hour my tea was refilled four times. I eventually got impatient and called Zhao Yue to ask her why she wasn't there yet.

She sounded distracted. 'I've got something on, I can't come. You go ahead and eat.'

My face clouded over. 'Hadn't we agreed to go out tonight?'

Zhao Yue apologised like a diplomat: 'I've really got something on so I can't come. Next time!'

'How come you're so busy?' I complained. 'What fucking business is so important?'

Zhao Yue sounded less apologetic now. 'What's the big deal? It's just dinner, right. So what if I can't come?' And she slammed down the telephone.

I almost exploded with anger. 'Screw her!' I said, flinging my phone to the ground. The attentive waitress picked it up. She said, 'Sir, you dropped your phone.' Looking at her concerned expression, my heart surged with sorrow. I thought if only Zhao Yue was so sweet and considerate. I removed the card from the flowers and ripped it up, thinking, you go ahead and eat. Eat your fill. Then I strode from the restaurant.

The waitress called after me: 'Sir, your flowers.'

I turned with a smile and said, 'You can have them,' then enjoyed her stunned expression.

CHAPTER SEVEN

After leaving the Jinjiang Hotel, I drifted along the bank of
the Funan River whose water was alight with reflections.
Loverrs wandered the river banks hand in hand, whispering softly in each other's ears. There was the sound of quiet
laughter.

Clearly Zhao Yue and I needed to talk. For around
a week now we'd been having these brutal fights which
could be triggered by a sentence, even a look. Often
they were unbearable, ripping open our scars and leaving them dripping with blood. At the height of my anger
I even wanted to try out kung fu on her. It didn't help
that Zhao Yue's main character flaw was her love of post-
mortems. Each time after a quarrel she demanded that we
clearly apportion responsibility: who said what; I said that
because you said that, etc. As a result, any time we had a

big argument we had to have a small argument afterwards. I said that the two of us were becoming like Cao Cao and Guan Yu: every three days a big fight, every five days a small fight.[7] Even when smiling, she was angry inside.

When Zhao Yue and I had first started dating she was caring and sorted out many things in my life. We would often take a walk around campus after dinner, hands entwined. The little wood, the hill, the grass behind the auditorium — all these had witnessed our laughter and tears. Once when I had a high fever, she stayed with me in the hospital for two days, hardly closing her eyes until my fever broke. She hit her head against a wall from sheer exhaustion. Thinking about this, I grieved. We'd had so much good feeling between us, so how had we got to where we were today?

Once, just before Spring Festival, we'd had a really spectacular bust-up which woke up everyone in the building. I said to her quite seriously, 'Forget it, there's no point in talking. We'll just divorce.'

'Good,' she said. 'Tomorrow we'll go to the divorce bureau.'

When dawn came, though, we both had second thoughts.

'Are we still going to the bureau?' I asked her.

She started to wail, and put her head in my lap, while using her hands to beat my chest. 'I'm not ready to lose you' … wah wah wah.

When I got home I made a pot of tea and planned my 're-education' of Zhao Yue. First, I would make her a voluntary confession of my faults. I had the script worked out: It was my fault, I shouldn't have lost my temper. You were right — it was just dinner. No big deal. What's more, I could have got you a takeaway instead.

After that I'd casually mention the flowers. The thought of that 268 yuan was painful, and Zhao Yue would surely be touched. Then I would strike while the iron was hot and introduce my central themes: tolerance, restraint, and understanding. As my main tactic I would rely on psychology: stress progress, encourage with praise, and make a little educational criticism in passing. And try not to lose it.

In order to create the right atmosphere, I dug out some mementos of our relationship. There was the lovers' yarn I gave her in 1997, the scarf she wove for me in 1998, and a set of handcuffs with keys bought during an outing to Qinghai Lake. Zhao Yue would sometimes demand I be handcuffed by her side before she would sleep. In addition, there were twenty-three letters, sixteen congratulations cards and two big piles of photos. She had copied all my poems into a black-spined notebook, choosing the title *Sent into Exile on a Dark Night*. On the title page she'd written the following inscription: *You love to read books. I love you, like a mouse loves rice.*

My memory has retained a clear image associated with that. Zhao Yue's head is raised, her gaze passionate, her expression solemn. With a slightly hurt look she is saying: If in the future you don't want me, I'll still have that book.

Zhao Yue didn't come home at all that night. Around 3 a.m. I couldn't stay awake and drifted off into a restless sleep. When I woke I heard upstairs playing Ren Xian Qi's 'Sad Pacific Ocean':

Forward one step and it's dusk
Backward one step and it's birth
From deep below the surface the past drifts up
Memories return, but you're already gone

My emotions were stirred up; I started crying and couldn't stop. I ran to the bathroom, where I suddenly noticed in the mirror that my face was still somewhat handsome.

This month the company's sales figures had unexpectedly dropped: compared with the same period the previous year they were down seventeen per cent. When the results came in I was dismayed. We'd always been the Sichuan and Chongqing area masters, especially when it came to petrol where almost no one could touch us. I'd bragged to Bighead Wang that if we were to suspend our service for just three months, there would be at least 100,000 cars in Sichuan out of action. Bighead Wang was impressed. 'You really are the dog's bollocks,' he told me. 'I'll just call you "car god", how about that?'

I called a sales team meeting to analyse what had gone wrong and work out a strategy. We talked it through for ages and everyone had their say. Gradually my ideas coalesced and I stood up and outlined my plan.

'Firstly, to fight off the upstart Lanfei brand, we'll

organise a big order meeting for the distributors and use up all their budgets for the year,' I said. 'Secondly, to counter any threat from the rest of Sichuan province's car factories we'll take action to increase sales, focusing on the final sales link. Thirdly, we will do a one-month advertising blitz on Sichuan TV, radio and internet platforms. It'll be a three-dimensional sales strategy.'

Finally I told Zhou Yan that before she went home she was to report to Head Office all the decisions reached at today's meeting.

'Do you want me to get Fatty Dong's signature?' she asked cautiously.

I glared and said bluntly, 'The prick knows nothing.'

I announced the end of the meeting. As I went out the door I was still cursing Zhou Yan for her stupidity. Why should I let other people get the credit for my achievements?

My remark got back to Fatty Dong. He came to find me in a fury, puffing out his cheeks like a toad. He said, 'You're too disrespectful to me, talking that way.'

I put on a charming expression and spouted some bullshit. Manager Dong, your specialty is administration. It's best if you don't interfere with marketing and sales.'

He went ballistic, and shouted for Zhou Yan. 'Without my signature, no one is allowed to distribute documents to Head Office,' he told her, then left in a huff.

Zhou Yan asked me what to do.

'Distribute the report,' I said. 'If the sky falls down I'll hold it up.'

Zhou Yan hesitated, then said in a small voice, 'You shouldn't antagonise him. Both of you will lose.'

Before the Spring Festival, Lanfei car oil company had head-hunted me and tried to lure me away with a high salary. I'd smiled ironically because I was more than willing to change jobs. I just didn't know how I could pay back the 200,000 yuan that I owed the company.

Whenever I thought about the money I got a headache. Our previous general manager had been a well-meaning old guy who didn't have any serious vices apart from lechery. He always followed my advice, and never asked questions. Now he'd been replaced by my mortal enemy Fatty Dong. From the moment we'd joined the company the two of us had been locked in both open and covert struggle. Now our hostility had the elemental force of fire and water. There was no way this jerk was going to let me off lightly. I had to find a way out of the situation myself.

On a whim I gave Li Liang a call and asked him about the futures market. He said the situation was very good. Not just quite good but extremely fucking good. In barely one month his account had got a 200,000 boost. I sounded him out, asking if you took 4 million and invested it in stocks how much could you earn in one month. The receiver made clicking sounds and I imagined Li Liang pressing buttons on a calculator. Eventually he said, If you invested well, you should have more than 10 million.

When I heard this, my heart thumped wildly.

My job title didn't sound like a big deal, but actually I had a lot of responsibility. Each month at least 2 million yuan passed through my hands. Company management was lax. Open a private account, divert a little in stages, and no one would have a clue. Bighead Wang and I shared the same view: if you had capital and didn't use it, that was the biggest waste.

Money—it really did make things happen. Last year I played around with a beautiful female student. She was one metre sixty-eight with a big front and prominent behind. Wildly seductive. I gave her a watch, a mobile phone, a Jaeger handbag, then finally tricked her into bed. One day in the Springtime Department Store, we saw a 3700 yuan Ports dress. She slipped it on and looked all the more delicately attractive. For some reason, though, when she pestered me to buy it, I suffered an attack of tight-fistedness. From that point on she wouldn't have anything to do with me and so all my hard work was wasted. It was too bad. At the time I'd thought, If I had a few million, do you think I couldn't hold onto a small-time prostitute like you?

I raised the futures idea with Bighead. He instantly doused me in cold water.

'Is your head full of shit? Don't try out these crazy ideas on me. Make the money, of course, what's wrong with that? But pay it back? It doesn't matter what you say, you'll never get it back in time.'

'I'll try my luck with a few tens of thousands first,' I said. 'That shouldn't be too much of a problem.'

'It's up to you,' he said, 'but best discuss it with Zhao Yue. She's much smarter than you.'

CHAPTER EIGHT

The Chengdu of twenty years ago was smaller and the Funan River was cleaner. I lived in a yard owned by the water and electricity bureau. As soon as school was out, my gang of thugs would get together to fight and raise hell, getting ourselves filthy. All my bad habits were cultivated at that time: selfishness, coldness, detachment and a gobful of bad language. One day when I'd stayed out pissing about until really late, my father cursed me. Back I came with the following riposte: 'Leave me alone, you bastard.' My father wasn't happy, and as a result my buttocks ached for a whole month.

A few years later I'd already started getting drunk, watching porn and stalking girls. As preparation for my future as a playboy, I put in plenty of hard slog. At that time Li Liang was still planting seeds in the fields of Meishan planti, and

Bighead Wang was lurking on Xian street corners filching lamb kebabs. Zhao Yue cried a lot because her parents were fighting. The people we were twenty years ago didn't know much about life. When the time came, however, we would be swept by the flood of city life into our preordained relationships of today.

Each time I went home, my mother's head had a few more white hairs. She was a retired doctor but her whole life had been devoted to serving my father and my sister and brother. She was never shy about offering her opinion. Sometimes I wondered whether at any point she'd ever thought about an affair. Could she have been the same as me, prepared to destroy everything for a fleeting moment of pleasure?

Seeing me walk in, the old woman feigned irritation and said, 'So you still know the way back.'

I laughed and embraced her. 'Your son is busy,' I told her.

'You always say you're so busy, but I never see you bringing me a grandson.'

Well, there it was: the very reason I didn't go home often. Each time, she'd ask me about a grandson as if I was a stud bull. The strange thing was that Zhao Yue and I hadn't used contraception for almost two years but her period always came regularly. At my mother's insistence we went for two check-ups at the Golden Bull Women's and Children's Hospital. Verdict: everything completely normal. The second time it was one of my mother's former underlings who examined us. She gave Zhao Yue a few pregnancy tips such as doing it in the missionary position with her arse raised. When we got home, Zhao Yue insisted on making love that way, but I lost interest halfway through.

I asked Mother where Pa was and she said, 'At your Uncle's Wang's house of course, playing chess.'

My father sucked at all board games. When I'd just started primary school he excitedly taught me Go.[8] Two months later I already had to be merciful to him. Later, after his retirement, he decided to attend an old people's Go class. There he somehow got the idea that he had mastered Go and he called me to urgently demand that I come home and play. That day he lost seven games, I won seven. In the final game Father was in a good position, but at the moment of victory he carelessly allowed my men to surround him in a pincer movement. Whatever he did there was no way out of the trap. He wanted to play the move again, but I wouldn't let him, and his indignation was something to behold. He slapped the board, cursing me in his Henan dialect. 'I see I've raised you for nothing, you swine. What's the meaning of this? Any time I want to take back a move, you won't let me.'

Zhao Yue was struggling not to laugh. As soon as we were out the door she cracked up and said, 'Your father is really sweet.'

After washing down the tofu skins Mother had made for me with Father's Mountain Cloud and Mist Tea, I felt my mood improve. Father always had a go at me, saying that I lived too recklessly, and I thought he was right. Happiness could take many forms, and stability was one of them. On my way home I considered whether I should go to the trouble of having a child, to make my life as 'beautiful as the wind and sun, no clouds for a thousand li'.

At three in the morning, Zhao Yue sat up and started sobbing in the dim shadows. It had been past two before I'd drifted off so I was more than usually irritated to be woken. I hissed that she must have a mental illness to be crying like a ghost in the dark. Ever since the time she'd stayed out all night, I had changed my tactics, implementing my special 'Three Nos' policy: No questions, no interest, and no being polite. Soon enough, I thought, she'd crack and tell me all. What I never imagined was that she would continue to be so detached, so seriously indifferent to her husband. This cold war continued for three days, the two of us living together in a phony peace, marred only by sexual frustration.

Actually, the sexual frustration part didn't really get to me. Before going to sleep, I would jerk off over some porn, and then afterwards sigh, thinking, let's see who can keep this up the longest. Do you really think you'll win?

Zhao Yue turned on the light. She leaned against the wall, shaking with sobs. I've never been able to bear seeing women cry, and as soon as I saw her, I started to shake too.

'What's up?' I said. 'Stop crying, OK?'.

Zhao Yue choked up. 'Chen Zhong, tell me the truth. Do you love me or not?'

All my years of experience with women have taught me not to give a straight answer to this question. You have to be evasive, because if you're not careful, any answer is wrong. If you say 'I love you', she'll say you answered too easily, you weren't sincere enough. If you say 'I don't love you' then you're sure to die.

'Why ask?' I countered. 'Is it so important whether or not I love you? You have your entrepreneur lover, what do you still want your poor husband for?'

She cradled my head and kept crying. Huge tears dripped onto my face. I was shocked and afraid that something terrible had happened. Zhao Yue was bad at faking. Whatever happened to her was always written clearly on her face. When she first came to Chengdu, I helped her unpack and unexpectedly turned up the photograph of a handsome male student. On the back were written these words: *For Yue: I hope this feeling lasts for ever.* I recognised the guy as one of our class's biggest morons. In his freshman year, he once dashed into our literature society meeting wanting to become a member. Li Liang asked him a few obscure questions then said apologetically, 'You should leave. Our literature society doesn't welcome peasants.'

The photo didn't necessarily mean anything, but reading those words on the back started a fire in my heart. I started to torture a confession out of her. Zhao Yue tried to wriggle out of it, but my eyes were like spotlights. She had no alternative but to own up, saying that the dickhead had asked her out a few times but she'd always turned him down. The last time, however, she felt a bit sorry for him and so agreed to go for a walk, during which he'd dragged her along by the hand the whole time. 'I swear on my mother's health, we definitely didn't do anything,' she told me.

Zhao Yue's parents had separated when she was a child and Zhao Yue had lived with her mother. I knew that she wouldn't causally invoke her mother's name.

I put on some clothes then told Zhao Yue, 'Whatever you've got to say, get on with it. I'm ready..'

She pinched my arm and said she knew me too well. 'You'd love it if I'd done something wrong. It would be a great opportunity to dump me.' Then she sobbed so violently I thought she might faint.

I smothered all tenderness and, feeling like my heart had turned to stone, I asked her: 'Are you telling me you've never had an affair?'

She wept and said, 'Never, never. At least, not right now.'

Suddenly, I felt a sharp pain. I took her in my arms and held her tightly against my chest, smelling the light, delicate fragrance of her hair.

The next morning we got up at 10 a.m. Zhao Yue's eyes were red, her smile bashful. It seemed like she was in a reasonable mood. I called Young Li in the HR department and said that I was taking today off. The little bastard was cheeky to me.

'Brother Chen, is this because you want to deflower some more virgins?'

'Screw you,' I said. 'Today I want to do my duty and be with my wife.'

He laughed and said, 'If you can't be good be careful.'

Zhao Yue finished gargling and came out of the bathroom looking like an entirely new woman. I kissed her and said, 'My wife is tasty.'

She returned me a cloying smile.

Hand in hand, we went out the door. In Yulin North Road we ate a delicious bowl of noodles with fried egg and shared a bottle of beer. When Zhao Yue went to the bathroom to re-apply her make-up, I took advantage and called Bighead's mobile.

'Bighead, this time you've got to help me.'

'You creep, just say what's up.'

I lowered my voice. 'Fuck it, Zhao Yue has a lover.'

CHAPTER NINE

When our monthly salaries were paid, I went to the ATM to use my card and discovered something wrong. My basic wage was 6000, and with sales commission on top I should have got around 8200. However, only 7300 had gone into my account. I asked the accountant to explain. He went through his books and said that in March I'd been absent two days, so they had deducted 900 yuan. I swore, then went to find Fatty Dong.

He was talking to Liu Three. Recently Fatty had been going all out to win people over to his side. He treated my underlings to meals and showered them with presents. According to Zhou Yan, he was making extravagant promises of promotions and other favours.

Last night at 10 p.m. she'd called me and said, 'Chen Zhong, guess where I am.'

I'd laughed, 'If not underneath someone, then surely on top of someone.'

She said piss off, she was in the Binjiang Hotel. Fatty Dong was courting her and Liu Three over dinner, hinting that they should 'leave darkness for light'. Liu Three had already pledged his loyalty. She couldn't bear to watch, and so she'd slipped out to the toilet to call me. She sounded worried. 'You should be careful, they're devious.'

For a moment I felt dazed, as if someone had hit my head. Quite honestly I'd never imagined that Liu Three would betray me. Right from his graduation that little bastard had learned his trade from me. Everything he knew I'd taught him; I was like a brother to him. Almost every few months I'd given him a raise, promoting him one step after another to manager so that he now supervised more than seventy people. If he'd really joined forces with Fatty Dong, then I was in big trouble.

Now seeing them both in Fatty's office, I remarked pointedly that they were obviously talking about something important. Liu Three blushed and he muttered, 'Brother Chen, I have to go. You chat with Boss Dong.'

I sat down and asked Fatty Dong, 'What's this about my staying away from work last month?'

He acted dumb, saying that everything was done according to the system.

That made me fly into a rage. 'When did I miss work?' I demanded.

He fixed me with a stare, then picked up the telephone and called Young Liu to come in.

'You explain to Manager Chen,' he told him.

Young Liu gave an embarrassed laugh. 'Brother Chen, on the twenty-fourth and twenty-seventh you didn't ask for leave but you didn't come to work either, and so we put you down as absent.'

Although Young Liu wasn't one of my people, he was honest and upright. When Fatty Dong wrote that slanderous letter about the former general manager and forced all the office staff to sign, only Young Liu refused. Walking home with him once, I asked him about it. He said his personal philosophy was to never get involved in other people's fights, and never make false accusations. This filled me with admiration.

My mind was clear today. For Fatty Dong this was a case of one stone, two birds. Young Liu and I were thorns in his side, so he'd be only too eager for the two of us to start feuding. This guy had studied political science at university and was a proficient scholar of fucking people over. He often said it was a waste for him not to be an official. So I managed to repress my fury and said, 'On the twenty-fourth and twenty-seventh I was away on client business. There is no basis for deducting my salary.'

He pinched in his waist and puffed out his chest like a big-shot and said that the company had a regulation. If you were going to be away from the office you should sign the appropriate form. 'You didn't fill in the form so there's nothing I can do.'

I smiled coldly. 'Do you have to treat matters so rigidly?'

He spread his hands and said, 'You broke the rules. We

would like to help but we can't.'

This was typical of the prick. He talked in such a sanctimonious way, when actually he was filthy inside. I slammed the door on my way out, causing all one hundred people in the office to look up.

Liu Three came to my office after that and asked me what to do about the Neijiang payments issue. I gave him a cigarette and said, 'Liu Three, how do I treat you?

'There's no need to ask that,' he said. 'Without you, where would I be today?'

As he spoke, his voice wavered and he appeared to be remembering all the kindness I'd shown him in the past. My mood lightened and I thought, good, Liu Three isn't a person devoid of gratitude. I smiled and said, 'Then what's this pledge of devotion you've made to Fatty Dong?'

He boiled over. 'That Zhou Yan is a troublemaker,' he said. 'Such a cheap person doesn't care about keeping face. Flirting with Fatty Dong and then daring to tell lies about me?'

'How did she flirt with him?' I asked.

He gave a mincing imitation of Zhou Yan's voice: 'Fatty Dong, you are mature and serious. You are the company's most fascinating man.'

When I heard this I felt sick to the teeth. Zhou Yan is cheap, I thought.

The longer I sat there in my office, the more furious I

got. Nine hundred yuan! Fatty Dong deserved to die—he shouldn't screw with me so casually. I thought up methods of revenge. I'd round up a few thugs to bash that oily fat face to a pulp; or fix his car so that he was in a fatal accident. I fantasised about slipping him a few heroin cigarettes so that he became an addict and his wife left him. If Fatty Dong had any intuition at all, he'd be a trembling wreck right now.

Bighead called, pulling me away from these pleasurable imaginings. He sounded drunk, and told me in a slurred voice that he had the telephone bills I'd asked for. When I'd told him that Zhao Yue was having an affair, Bighead was outraged. He said he'd always known I should have stayed away from this kind of woman, 'Cheap bitch!'

Hearing this, I reflected that the business of sex really did get people upset. However, for the moment I was willing to believe that Zhao Yue had got carried away on just the one occasion. What was more, an affair was just my guess, not something I'd seen with my own eyes. Still, I had to admit that women were often better than men at hiding such things. In our third year at university Li Liang had a girlfriend from Chongqing called Su Xin. Although nothing special to look at, she had a hot body. Her personality was completely uninhibited and she said 'bollocks' even more often than I did. One time, the four of us were eating and Su Xin said to Li Liang, 'Even if we were caught together in the dorm, I'd still jump up and shout, "No, it hasn't gone in yet!"'

Zhao Yue had looked disapproving then, but I believed

she secretly shared Su Xin's philosophy of never confessing to your crimes.

I'd asked Bighead Wang to get a copy of Zhao Yue's mobile phone records. My thinking was that if Zhao Yue had got carried away just the once I could forgive her, but I needed to have all the facts. Otherwise I ran the risk of being a real jerk.

Bighead, however, had urged me to confront Zhao Yue. 'Can you really put up with this?' he asked. 'Are you a man or not?'

When he said that, I didn't have anywhere to hide. I vaguely began to hate him.

Bighead's precinct was located downtown. When I got there I discovered a riot. Two guys were handcuffed at the bottom of a stairwell, and there was a group of old bound-feet women making a fuss. I listened for a while before I worked out that the two guys were laid-off workers. They drove those illegal three-wheeled cars known in Chengdu as 'cake ears' and had been carrying passengers without the proper licence. When the city officials confiscated the vehicle, the two laid-off workers hadn't shown any remorse. Instead they'd started pushing and shoving, and so the cops had arrested them and brought them here. Siding with the two workers, the elderly women had followed the party all the way to the police station, demanding with some choice local dialect that the police give them justice.

Bighead was hiding in his office playing Mine-sweeper. Seeing me come in he let out a big sigh. 'In these lawless times, there are bad people everywhere,' he said.

'You're bad too,' I replied. 'Are people trying to better themselves through their own efforts really any of your business?'

Bighead claimed that orders had come from above. Then he slapped down a thick pile of paper and said, 'Investigate for yourself. This is a complete record of all the calls your wife's made in the past year.'

I didn't know whether the stack of paper was a disaster or a blessing. It was hard to concentrate. Outside the door was a seething cauldron of noise. Seeing Bighead Wang's concerned expression, I suddenly asked myself whether I really did want to know about this. Once I knew, what then? How would I cope with the secret concealed inside that stack of paper?

Projecting my mind through Chengdu's concrete jungle and chaotic traffic, I pictured Zhao Yue on her way home: the front of her skirt was dancing, her long hair was flying in the breeze. She still had the kind of beauty that moved people. But from this point on, were the two of us heading in the same direction?

Bighead Wang handed me a tissue and patted my shoulder.

'Don't feel down,' he said. 'When you get home, have a good talk to her. If you need me to do anything, feel free to ask.'

When I got home, though, I was met by an unexpected sight. Zhao Yue appeared from the kitchen wearing an apron. She smiled at me.

'Guess what I've made you for dinner?'

I sniffed and said, 'Bamboo shoots fried with beef, water-boiled fish, and my favourite, chestnut carbonado.'

She punched me. 'You greedy bastard, you guessed right.'

We ate dinner together. Zhao Yue had studied with my mother and her cooking had come on in leaps and bounds. The beef was succulent but not greasy, the fish fresh and tender, the chestnuts clean with a honeyed texture, the chicken sweet and crisp. When I was done, I let out a long sigh.

After dinner, Zhao Yue took me around the house and showed me how everything had been polished and our clothes neatly ironed. In the bedroom was displayed one of our wedding photos. There was a lipstick mark on the glass — right over my face.

Tender feelings overwhelmed me. Zhao Yue leaned against the door, smilingly watching me. Suddenly I threw her on the bed and ripped roughly at her clothes. She pushed me away, chuckling. Later, though, she grabbed my hand, drunk with desire, yelling out loudly without the least inhibition. We made crazy love to a soundtrack of the All-China News At Seven mixed with the sound of running water from next door.

Afterwards, Zhao Yue rubbed her face against my chest as I rolled down from the heights of carnal desire. The universe was empty. I lay in a damp patch, outwardly still and peaceful, but somehow anxious. Some lines of poetry from years ago dripped through my head:

> *A night years later,*
> *You cover your face and cry,*
> *The light of youth sometimes seems near, sometimes far.*
> *Who gave you a lifetime of doubt?*
> *Who was true and stands in the same place?*
> *Who is in heaven?*
> *Who is in hell?*
> *Who still searches for you in their dreams?*

Regret welled up in me and I felt like crying. Zhao Yue held me tightly in her arms, the light in her eyes as clear as water. In my memory a few things came together. I had a vision of meeting her seven years before on the steps of the library, a book under her arm as she approached me.

'Do you ever stop working?' I asked.

She lowered her head slightly but had a smile on her face.

I said, 'There's someone who'd like to go for a drink with you, but doesn't know whether you'd agree?'

She smiled, pressed her book against my chest, and said, 'Who's the shy one? Let's go!'

We looked at each other solemnly. Slowly the corners of her mouth curved into a smile. The smile widened and then there came an unexpected snorting sound. Without knowing why, we both started laughing. Our laughter was loud and hearty. Absorbed in the present we embraced on the bed, stroking each other until a certain part of my body rose.

Just then my mobile rang. It was Zhou Yan.

'Chen Zhong, how can you treat people this way?' she asked with a sigh.

'What do you mean?' I asked.

'Fatty Dong came here and accused me of being a traitor. I tell you, I never thought you'd sell me out like that. Are you even human?'

Then came the thud of the receiver being slammed down.

Zhao Yue asked me what was up but I ignored her. I dialled Liu Three's mobile and he didn't answer. I persisted, then finally heard his thin voice. I asked him to explain.

He hesitated a while, then said, 'Brother Chen, there's something I've always wanted to ask you.'

I gnashed my teeth. 'So, ask.'

'When Fatty Dong wrote the letter smearing Boss Sun, you knew all about it. Why didn't you stop it, or at least warn him?'

This was something I'd long regretted myself. At the time of plotting his coup, Fatty Dong had said to me, 'Old Sun is a waste of space. If we got rid of him, everyone would benefit.'

I'd seen this as an opportunity for me too, and so I'd allowed him free rein to set up Old Sun. From start to finish I didn't intervene.

I said to Liu Three, 'So that's the reason you've got together with Fatty Dong to screw me.'

He didn't reply.

'Come over here if you dare. Let's talk face to face.'

He said that as things had come to this, there was no need to talk any more.

I went ballistic. 'Fuck your mother, Liu Three!'

He laughed. 'Brother Chen, my mother's already old. I'll help you find a couple of younger chicks.'

CHAPTER TEN

Li Liang's wedding was a Chengdu sensation. On 1 May, twenty gleaming cars, arranged like words in a sentence, set off from Jinxiuu Gardens and cruised smoothly towards the Binjiang Hotel. We'd arranged things with the cops so there weren't any hold-ups. I was at the very front of the motorcade, driving a Mercedes-Benz 320. A little tune danced around in my head, a Zhonghua cigarette dangled from my lips, and when I saw a red light I accelerated just like a young punk. Li Liang sat at my side with a solemn expression. In his 30,000 yuan Zegna suit he looked very cool.

I teased him. 'Li Liang, my son, today you're marrying your wife. What's with the serious face?'

He didn't smile, just asked earnestly, 'Why do I feel a little frightened?'

'What's there to be frightened of?' I said. 'Ye Mei won't

bite you; at the most she'll give you a blow job.'

He laughed and shook his fist. But he soon became solemn again and sighed loudly, apparently weighed down with anxiety.

Having been chief witness to Li Liang's golden years I was familiar with every one of his former girlfriends. Even their bra sizes. Don't get the wrong idea—it was Li Liang who told me. In second semester of our first year at university he fell big time for a Jiangsu girl in the PE department. She had a classically beautiful face—large eyes, red lips, fair complexion, straight nose—but her figure … well, it was grotesque. Her lower arms were the width of my calf, her upper arms bloated and her midriff well-padded. She had what was known as a 'tiger back' and a 'bear waist'. There was a story that some guy had tried to rob her in the dining hall and she'd fought back. Before long the guy's strength was spent and he sat on the floor and started crying. He refused to get up, as if she'd put a spell on him. This girl liked to go for a long run every morning and had the force of ten thousand horses all galloping together. The two magnificent constructions on her chest moved backwards and forwards like an ocean swell. It was an overwhelming sight. One evening when we were chatting after lights out in our dormitory, Chen Chao from Shandong slapped his hand on the edge of the bed and expressed his admiration and reverence for that imposing chest: 'Mother, those are quite simply two Mount Tais.'[9]

After that, the name 'Mount Tai' got around fast. I didn't know exactly what Li Liang loved about Mount Tai, but I

believed this love was the real thing. Each night when Li
Liang returned from a date, he dragged me to the steam
room to report on how they'd held hands, how they'd
kissed, how Li Liang had used his hands to 'climb Mount
Tai'. There wasn't anything he wouldn't tell me.

Li Liang was a talent in those days and threw himself
into things with great passion. Every day he'd write a few
'against the current, hold you in my arms' type of romantic poems, which made Bighead Wang completely despise
him. When no one was around Bighead would ask: 'Has
this asshole Li Liang got water in his brain?'

When the summer holiday came that year, Mount Tai
returned to her home town of Nanjing. We saw her off at
the train station. The two of them shed tears, held hands
and stared into each other's eyes. I felt like cracking up
but restrained myself. When the train started, Mount Tai
waved forlornly from inside the carriage. No one could
have foreseen what happened next. Li Liang suddenly
took off like a leopard, sprinting after the train, slamming
his hand against the window and shouting himself hoarse:
'Little Zhu, I love you. I LOVE YOU!'

His voice boomed down the platform, making heads
turn. Finally, about a hundred metres away from where
I was standing, he threw himself to the ground with a
dramatic thud. I ran over to where he lay completely
motionless, blood trickling from his head.

When you tell your dream to ten thousand people
The dream will grow wings.

—Li Liang, 'Love'

Surprisingly through, they broke up straight after the holiday. Li Liang wouldn't say why, just smoked cigarettes and looked depressed. The next few girlfriends all went the same way—none lasted more than three months. Secretly I started to wonder whether Li Liang had some sort of sexual problem. Once, in the dormitory, I had stayed up all night reading a book, then at dawn stealthily climbed onto Li Liang's bunk to get a cigarette. He'd appeared to be asleep, but when he heard me he jumped abruptly. His face was very white and he looked shocked out of his wits. I realised that he'd been jerking off.

Some people, like Li Liang, can sacrifice a lot for love. I both respect and despise these people. My own feelings are more complex. I have always viewed love as a game. No one *really* loves; or, to put it another way, we only really love ourselves.

After he split with Mount Tai, Li Liang became mentally and spiritually unstable. Sometimes he'd go missing for half the night. Bighead Wang and I went out looking for him once, and eventually found him sitting in a small wood opposite the female students' dorm. He sat facing Mount Tai's window, and whistling a tuneless melody. I was about to call out to him, but Bighead grabbed me. At that moment the moonlight shifted like water, sprinkling the wood with silver, and we saw two fat tears navigating the contours of Li Liang's face.

Li Liang still missed Mount Tai, I thought, all these

years later as I hit the accelerator. Nevertheless, his life was definitely better than mine. He earned good money, he had status and he understood all the big questions of life. Whereas deep inside I was still stuck where I'd been years ago: a shy first-year student wearing a 5 yuan T-shirt.

At the wedding banquet I tried my best to lighten things up. I asked Ye Mei, 'Are you willing to accept Li Liang as your husband?'

Ye Mei nodded, but then I continued: 'Are you ready, come wind, come rain, thunder or lightning, come warm winters or cold summers, to always love him, comfort him and screw him?

Everyone else laughed. Ye Mei glared. I thought of that wild night in the hotel at Leshan when she hadn't spoken to me for a long time.

The bride and groom did the rounds of the tables making toasts. Bighead indicated a big plate filled with seven or eight kinds of dishes, and asked Ye Mei to make a calculation.

Tell me, how many dishes on each plate, he said.[10]

Ye Mei hesitated for a while then said, 'One plate ... one plate, seven dishes.'

The whole table collapsed with laughter. Zhao Yue leaned against me and laughed until she was gasping for breath.

I said, 'Li Liang, you stud ... seven times a night ... such stamina.'

This set everyone laughing helplessly again. Ye Mei

seemed slow to get the joke, but then quite suddenly she picked up a wine glass and hurled its contents in my face. The 800-yuan-a-bottle wine dripped down my chest towards my stomach. I leapt to my feet, Bighead's gaping mouth filling my vision.

What happened after that was a blur, but the whole room was shocked. Zhao Yue helped me wipe the wine from my face, while Bighead jumped up indignantly, then stood there not knowing what to do. Ye Mei, her face very red, still clutched the glass, and I noticed that Li Liang was staring at me with a strange smile. It seemed to me that he was considering something. I licked my lips: it was a bordeaux with a sweet flavour and a slightly sour aftertaste.

No one was in the mood to party after that. Bighead Wang muttered a few stuttering sentences into the microphone and the wedding wound up.

On the way home Zhao Yue stared silently out of the car window. I deliberately drove too fast, wanting to provoke her, but from the moment she got in the car to when we got home she didn't even look at me.

Finally I said, 'What's up?'

She was lying fully clothed on the bed and didn't reply, instead clawing over and over at the wall with her fingers. When I hugged her, she struggled silently.

'What's wrong? At least say something,' I told her.

'What is our relationship?' she muttered.

I laughed angrily and said, 'It's more than just *a relationship*. You're my wife!'

'Seems like you're more interested in someone's else's

wife,' she said.

Suddenly I was worried. 'What do you mean?'

Zhao Yue met my eyes fearlessly. 'You tell me.'

I was nervous now. Feigning indignation I turned away and spat out, 'You're crazy.'

Zhao Yue ignored me, continuing to scratch at the wall. I sat there dumbly until I thought of something, and then I hurried downstairs two and three steps at a time. At the public telephone opposite the entrance to our stairwell, I made a call.

A male voice answered. 'Who do you want?'

'Zhao Yue,' I said.

He seemed surprised and asked, 'Who's there?'

'I'm Zhao Yue's husband. Who are you?'

He was silent, then the line went dead. After a moment I called Zhao Yue's mobile phone, but got the following repeated message: *The subscriber you want is busy. Please wait and try again.*

I smiled coldly.

My head stung with resentment. I called Bighead and invited him out for a drink, but he said he wanted to sleep. We could go drinking another day. I noticed that he seemed a bit fed up with me. Next I tried Zhou Weidong, but he said he was visiting Qingcheng Mountain and wouldn't be back until the day after tomorrow. Finally, I called my brother-in-law's mobile. He swore at me. Apparently, the day before there had been a family dinner and everyone had waited for me to turn up but I didn't show.

The old woman muttered to herself the whole night, he said.

I hung up. A few fire engines rushed past. Apart from that the night was peaceful. From one apartment there came the sound of laughter, from another the sound of crying. Standing in the shadows, where no light reached, I felt myself smiling but I wasn't happy.

A taxi slowed nearby and the driver gave me a questioning look. I nodded, opened the door and got in.

'Where are we going?' he asked.

'Find me a good place to have some fun.'

'What kind of fun?' he asked.

'Girls.'

'Try Longtan, One Fifty Street,' he said, 'there are loads of girls there, both beautiful and cheap.'

'Great,' I said. 'Take me to Longtan, One Fifty Street.'

CHAPTER ELEVEN

The taxi stopped in front of a wall plastered with billboard health warnings about gonorrhoea and syphilis. I handed the driver a fifty, and he asked if I needed him to wait. I said no, I'd be there all night.

The name One Fifty Street referred to the price. For 150 yuan you could get anything. There were around seventy to eighty KTV parlours[11] on both sides of the street, all with tacky coloured lights around the doors. Hideous drunken singing came from inside: sounds like roaring bulls and whinnying horses. Dozens of girls sat outside each place, smiling through their disguise of powder and youth.

Slowly I walked down the street. From each side, fluent patter assailed my ears. It could be a romantic pitch: 'Come on, handsome, I love you.' A shrewd appeal to profit:

'Beautiful girls and reasonable prices, only an idiot would say no.' Or it might tout sexual proficiency: 'Sir, come and play here. Our girls are good at it!'

One misshapen runt kept following me and pushing his establishment: 'All our girls are fifteen or sixteen, fresh and tender. Come on, come on.'

I shook off his hand and walked on, still checking out the girls on both sides of the street. My mobile rang: it was Zhao Yue. I cut her off but she kept calling, so I turned off my phone.

It was me who bought Zhao Yue her first ever mobile phone. 1 May 1997, four years ago to the day. At that time the Motorola Gc87c cost more than 5000 yuan. Zhao Yue thought this was too expensive and didn't want it, until I set her straight.

'You think I bought this for your benefit? Take it, dimwit! It's just so I can check up on you more easily.'

Zhao Yue reluctantly accepted the phone, but in the first months she rarely turned it on. Her monthly call fee was even lower than the plan costs. She didn't become a fully paid-up member of the sect of mobile phone users until she got promoted and her new position included a 150 yuan monthly mobile subsidy.

My head was still spinning from the call I'd made earlier. That number had appeared regularly in her list of calls in the last two months—the greatest frequency nine times a day, the longest duration one hour seventeen minutes. I'd checked the date of that call and it was the very day I'd bought her those roses. While they were talking, I'd been waiting at home for my wife to come back, wondering how to apologise to her.

The past two days I'd exhausted myself helping with Li Liang's wedding. I'd organised the loan of military cars, gone back and forth about the banquet, written and sent out invitations, decorated the bridal chamber. Being so busy had helped keep my mind off the situation. All the same, whenever I had time I couldn't help wondering where they met, where they slept together. Whether Zhao Yue moaned underneath that guy like she did with me. What was weird was that instead of getting angry, I just felt sad. The night before, after a few drinks, I'd stood in front of the window for a while in a sort of daze. Li Liang had sensed something wrong and tried to ask me what, but I'd evaded the issue.

I regretted making that phone call. If it hadn't been for that, everything might have gone back to normal. I could have chosen to believe I was just being paranoid and performed the necessary mental contortions to accept whatever explanation Zhao Yue made. No matter that I would have suspected her for the rest of my life. But now this stranger had appeared and the distance between Zhao Yue and me had suddenly grown. We were colder, estranged. It was as if there were tens of thousands of miles between us.

A moon-faced girl pulled my arm, rubbing against me with her voloptuous breasts. 'Hey, good-looking, you're handsome. I want to love you.'

I smiled and reflected coldly how cheap love was that you could get such a generous amount for only 150 yuan. In her favour though, she did have a beautiful round arse which felt good when I gave it a quick rub. I followed her into a dimly lit room. She took off her clothes then lay on the bed smiling at me. I buried my head in her breasts and held her, thinking that if Zhao Yue died right then I wouldn't care at all.

Coming downstairs together afterwards, the girl put on a show of being sweet. She clung to me and called me 'hubbie'. Unexpectedly, this made me mad.

'Fuck you! Who's your husband?' I snapped.

She stared at me, shocked. 'Cheap bitch,' I said, and went out the door. Behind my back I heard her shouting after me, something like, 'Fuck your mother.'

I turned on my mobile to check the time. Midnight already. The street was full of cars. This was when many Chengdu men, having stuffed themselves with food and drink, came out to work off some excess energy. How many tales of cruel youth had unfolded on this uneven street amid the colourful lights and the music, the powder and the condoms? I sighed and suddenly felt hungry, remembering that I'd hardly eaten anything at the wedding dinner. When Ye Mei threw the wine over me, I hadn't even had a single mouthful of the specially cooked hairy crab.

Zhao Yue called yet again. This time, after a moment's hesitation, I took the call. When she asked me what I was up to, I told her I was out whoring.

'I know you've got some misunderstandings about me,' she said. 'Come back and we'll talk about it.'

'I haven't come yet,' I told her, 'so you'll just have to wait.'

She called me shameless and hung up.

I felt good again; thinking about Zhao Yue's angry face gave me a happy glow. There were a few small restaurants along the street. Going into one, I ordered two bottles of beer, some cold dishes and a serve of twice-cooked pork. I ate with great relish, reflecting that right now Bighead Wang would be sleeping with his wife, while Li Liang might be doing it with Ye Mei. At the thought of Li Liang, though, I felt guilt again. Holding up my glass, I addressed the fading lights of Chengdu: 'Li Liang, my brother, please forgive me. Had I known Ye Mei was your woman, I wouldn't have done her to save my life.'

The hole-in-the-wall restaurant was unhygienic. While I was eating the meat dish I found a long hair. Feeling disgusted, I turned around to spit. As I did, I noticed a dark-green Honda Accord slowly cruising along the street. Fatty Dong was at the wheel, his fat neck craning as he inspected the merchandise. Quickly draining my glass, I went outside and watched him drive past the venues one by one. Finally he stopped outside a KTV place called Red Moon.

Fatty Dong had a typical official's face: fat, round cheeks and large ears but somehow dignified in appearance. In contrast, his wife was dried-up and ugly enough to scare people. Once I'd seen them on the street together; his wife stalked along in front with a cigarette in her mouth; Fatty Dong followed her like a pet pig, servile and obedient, an expression of reverence on his face. On 8 March last year, International Women's Day, Fatty Dong had turned up two hours late with bruises and cuts on his face and neck, bleary-eyed, as if he'd just been crying. I guessed his wife must have beaten him up.

Finding Fatty Dong's home number in my address book, I hit the dial button with a big grin.

His wife's dour voice answered, 'Who is it?'

Just as I was about to reply, inspiration struck. I ended the call immediately, ran to the public phone and pressed three digits: 110.

The duty cop sounded cute. She asked me what was wrong and in a low whisper, I told her I suspected someone was dealing drugs. Recently the cops had received loads of publicity for their campaign against drug crime, and it was said that a drug squad hero from Xichang had just been transferred here. In fact, only the week before, a high school mate of Li Liang's who'd opened a spicy soup restaurant, was caught buying 250 jin of poppy shells at Lianhua Pond market. Li Liang had wanted to stand bail for him but Bighead advised him against it. 'Whatever you do, don't get involved,' he'd shouted. 'Drugs are the hottest crime right now, and whoever gets messed up with them will fry.'

As soon as she heard the word 'drugs' the cop got excited and she quizzed me in detail about the location and distinguishing features of the suspect. I told her the approximate location, then gave her Fatty Dong's car registration and said I hadn't seen his face clearly.

'He's really fat and wearing a purple shirt,' I said. 'The gear's on him or maybe concealed in his car tyre.'

She pressed me for my name and ID number but I pretended to be scared. 'Please don't ask,' I said. 'I wouldn't have called the cops if I'd known you'd want my details.'

I particularly enjoyed setting this trap for Fatty Dong because I'd had some similar misfortune myself on a business trip to Mianyang in 1999. I'd just undressed when there was a knock at the door. Somehow I sensed it meant something bad. Immediately I grabbed my pants and pulled them back on. But the greater the hurry, the more mistakes you make. Somehow I put them on back to front. Just as I was about to rectify the situation, the door was kicked open and two ferocious cops dashed in. I almost fainted, but the prostitute managed to hold me up. I was fined 4000 yuan. Fortunately I'd had enough money on me, otherwise things might have escalated.

I hung up feeling great. On second thoughts, however, I decided not to let Fatty Dong off so cheaply. The fine for visiting a prostitute was a few thousand yuan, which was insignificant to him. I needed to be more ruthless: if you don't beat a snake to death you'll be bitten by it. After some thought, I decided to call my brother-in-law. He edited the gossip section of a tabloid newspaper and every day he published ridiculous news about things like a double-headed snake appearing somewhere or a rooster that had just laid a double-yolk egg. I called him Na Wuo, after a likeable idiot character in a sitcom played by actor Feng Gong. My brother-in-law was easy-going and would smile back at me saying, 'You baby. You're always taking the piss out of me, but you never give me any stories.'

My brother-in-law had been asleep and sounded irritable when he answered the phone. I got straight to the point.

'I've got a lead for you. A drug dealer out whoring at night and the cops turning out in force to arrest him.'

At once he became alert. I gave him the details and he said he'd send a hack to investigate the story.

'You'll have to hurry,' I said, 'or the guy'll be nabbed by the cops.'

He said OK. Just as he was about to hang up, I muttered hesitantly, 'Brother-in-law …'

'What?' he said.

I thought for a moment, then decided to level with him.

'You have to publish this guy's photo in the paper.'

'Is he your enemy?' he asked.

'Yeah. And if you don't help me, then I'm done for.'

After the call with my brother-in-law, I hailed a taxi on the street and said to the driver, 'Take me to Chengdu.'

He asked how much I'd pay. I told him 200 yuan then got into the car. After that I dialled Fatty Dong's home number again.

'Dong Guang is whoring in Longtan,' I informed his wife.

CHAPTER TWELVE

In 1996, Zhao Yue and I had gone to Emei Mountain[12] where we came across a stinky fortune-telling Taoist at Fuhu Temple. The guy smelt as if he'd just crawled out of a sewer. Zhao Yue was usually a big fan of sanitation, but that day she insisted we should let him tell our fortune. After talking some bullshit he told us that we would break up because we'd been enemies in a previous life. Zhao Yue believed him and turned pale, asking if there was any way we could avoid this fate. As he rubbed his greasy grey goatee, there was an evil look in his eyes. He said he'd help us if we paid him 200 yuan. Against my strong opposition Zhao Yue handed over 200 yuan from her bag. That was half her basic monthly salary and I was fuming. The Taoist gave her a black piss-pot-like jar, saying it was a saint's jar that could drive away ghosts and repel demons. Sneering, I

asked if it had once contained the urine of Laozi,[13] creator
of the world. Zhao Yue gave me a kick for my blasphemy.

On our way back to Chengdu Zhao Yue acquired a
new nickname from me: Pisspot Master. I joked that she
belonged to the third generation of the E-Mei school and
was so strong that she could catch one of Britain's mad
cows with her bare hands. She stared tearfully out the window. When I asked what was wrong, she said something
that moved me deeply.

'It doesn't matter if it works or not, Chen Zhong. You
know that what I want isn't this jar but your heart.'

I patted her hand and comforted her. 'Don't worry, my
heart is in this jar.'

For about a year after that she bowed and muttered to
that pot every two weeks. I mocked her superstition, but got
glares and punches in reply. Finally I couldn't put up with
it any longer and 'accidentally' dropped the jar. Zhao Yue
cried, claiming I'd broken it on purpose. From then on, she
brought it up every time we quarrelled.

As I climbed our stairwell that night, I was thinking that
even if that jar hadn't been broken, there was no way for
any of us to avoid fate. Fate seldom listened to me. When
it came to the crunch moments, it listened to God. It
reminded me of 'Zhao's Family Rules', drawn up by Zhao
Yue shortly after we got married, namely: 'Tiny things can't
be decided by Zhao Yue, while big things can't be decided
by Chen Zhong.'

According to Zhao Yue's guidelines, only the first three
reports on the evening national news counted as 'big

things'. In those early days she'd read out her 'rules' every night before bed, and then jump into my arms, laughing just like a kid. When did we forget those 'rules'? At what point had our life together lost its hope, its caring, playing and laughing?

The TV was on but the screen was a snowstorm. A harsh sound came out of the speakers. I was irritated: why hadn't she turned the TV off? I did a tour of the whole apartment and found all the lights on but nobody there. Where was she?

The balcony door was wide open and I shivered as I felt the cold wind from outside. Looking down, I saw only endless night outside. All the hairs on my body stood on end. Had Zhao Yue jumped?

In our last year of university, there'd been an aura of death hanging over our group. First Zhang Jun from Qiqihaer who lived in the dorm opposite died of lymph cancer. When his girlfriend came to collect his stuff she cried until she fainted. Then, one beautiful spring night, Qi Yan, a talented girl, jumped from the sixteenth floor of the teaching building. Her corpse was smashed and bloody. Qi Yan was idolised by most of the guys in our dorm. She looked like the film star Rosamund Kwan and was good at singing, playing the piano and hosting parties. It was a true pleasure dancing with her. The day before she died, she sat with us in the canteen, picking the slices of greasy fatty meat from her meal and dumping them on the table. When I said it was a waste, Qi Yan glared at me and said, 'If you want to eat them, just take them.'

I was about to answer back, but Zhao Yue stepped heavily on my foot so I shut up at once. The next day Qi Yan killed herself. She was three months pregnant, it was said.

During our last month at university, we all felt that our lives were like dreams. Alcohol, mahjong or tears: the empty days flashed by. Li Liang wrote a poem:

You dissipate
Your smile blooming at dawn's feast
What God owes you
Is recorded
What you owe to God
Must be paid back sooner or later

I understood. Somehow we'd started to believe that nothing in the rest of our lives mattered. The main task of life was to be happy. God would break that jar at the moment of truth, and we would not care if the final scene was happy or sad.

Now I was scared and worried. When I called Zhao Yue's mobile, it rang forlornly beside her pillow. Her bag was there too, and her lipstick lay on the dresser, reminding me of her red lips that had kissed me many times. It started drizzling outside and I felt like I was in an abyss.

Finally I took a torch downstairs, fully prepared to find her corpse. As I passed the apartment building entrance, I saw something skulking in the dark. My scalp was prickling with pins and needles, but I mustered up the courage to check it out. In the circle of light from my torch, my Zhao Yue, sat propped against the wall. Her eyes swum with tears and there was a bottle of spirits beside her.

I dropped the electric torch and hugged her. I thought you'd died!

Zhao Yue wept, giving off a strong smell of alcohol. The torch rolled on the ground, illluminating raindrops.

I took Zhao Yue upstairs and washed her hands and feet, put a hot towel on her forehead, then watched her fall deep into sleep like a child. The rain stopped and there was a sweet smell of flowers. The smell was fucking good, I thought. Dawn was about to break, and on this sleepless morning I watched the sky gradually turn pale.. Zhao Yue still loved me; everything was cool.

It was 1 May 2001 — the day my best friend got married; the day I went whoring; the day my enemy's luck ran out. It was the day my wife got drunk and cried, the day I thought she'd killed herself. Now, at dawn, a white fog hung over the city, making it look surreal.

I boiled some porridge and smoked a cigarette, smirking.

But you never know what's going to happen next. At 7:50 a.m. my mother called and said in an alarmed voice, Come home now. Your father is dying.

CHAPTER THIRTEEN

Whenever I returned to Chengdu during my student days, Father picked me up at the railway station. He wasn't one for talking much. When he saw me he'd just smile and say, 'How did you let your hair get so long? It's a mess.'

I protested that I wasn't a two-year-old who couldn't find his way home, and he didn't have to pick me up at all. The real reason I hated him coming was that he always used my nickname, Baby Rabbit, in front of Li Liang and others. This was embarrassing. Once, after we'd dropped off Li Liang, I howled at my father, 'Baby Rabbit, Baby Rabbit! Remember, my name is Chen Zhong. Chen Zhong!'

He stared at me with a hurt expression, then lowered his head and didn't say anything for ages.

My father had a deformed right foot, which manifested itself as a limp while walking. Because of this I never wanted him to visit me at the university. In my second year, he went to the coastal resort of Beidaihe[14] to convalesce and on his way through stopped by the school. At the moment he showed up, I'd just put my head down to sleep after playing mahjong right through the night. As soon as I saw him I felt pissed off, fearing that yet again he'd embarrass me. Sure enough when my father came in he acted up, handing round cigarettes, and calling Bighead Wang 'comrade'. I was so mortified that I almost forcibly dragged him away. I didn't even invite him to stay for a meal. My father left feeling bruised, but when he got to Beidaihe he called to remind me to 'live a more regular life'.

Standing in the corridor at the hospital, I felt sad as I thought of my father back then waiting for me at the train station. Zhao Yue was quietly comforting my mother. The old woman had been crying since morning, when she'd found my father collapsed in the bathroom. All the way to the hospital she'd sobbed until her eyes were red. I suddenly wondered whether, when it came down to it, there would be anyone to cry for me in the way my mother was for my father.

My brother-in-law called. He said that he and my sister would be there soon. He added: 'I've done what you asked me to do. Buy a paper.'

Fatty Dong looked ridiculous in the newspaper photograph. His mouth was half open and his hands were raised high. He looked like a nationalist general who'd decided to go over to the other side. The only disappointment was that his eyes were blocked out so you couldn't clearly see his expression. My brother-in-law had gone to town, putting the story on the front page under the headline: *Illegal Couple Apprehended, Huge Commotion*. I read ithe colourful article right through. It said that once Fatty Dong realised there was something wrong he'd leapt from the second-floor window in a vain attempt to make a getaway and was seized at once by cops waiting in ambush. Below the article was a 600-word editorial written by my brother-in-law with the headline *A Technical Analysis of Whoring*. It said: *Given the current policy of cracking down on pornography, those who visit prostitutes had better practise kung fu. Otherwise it will be hard for them to avoid capture.*

I was esctatic that Fatty Dong's day of reckoning had finally come. But when I went back to the emergency room and saw my mother crying, my pain returned.

My mother had given birth to two sons but my elder brother died of pulmonary tuberculosis at the age of three. When I arrived she was afraid that I would fail to reach manhood too. Her solution was to give me a childhood name that wouldn't attract fate's attention: Baby Rabbit. She also stuffed me with every kind of pill. I reckoned that if my stomach had had the ability to store them, by now I'd have more than enough to open a drug store. My fourth grade primary school teachers were rather surprised by an essay I wrote entitled 'A Small Matter' which related an incident in which my mother gave me an injection in my butt without even knowing what was wrong with me.

Zhao Yue was comforting my mother in a soft voice while holding my hand. Warmth passed from her smooth, warm skin into my hand, and from there to my heart.

A pretty nurse approached and asked whether we were Chen Zhenyuan's family. Standing up nervously, I asked how my father was. She smiled and said, 'Don't worry, there's nothing seriously wrong with your father. You can go and complete the hospital registration process.'

I was overjoyed and couldn't help crying out to my mother: I knew the old man would be okay. It was just you making a big fuss.

The old lady slowly smiled, as if she was just waking from a dream.

There was a problem: I wasn't carrying enough cash. I'd set out with 1200 yuan on me, and after the taxi, registration and emergency treatment fees we were 500 yuan short. Zhao Yue searched through her pockets but only found 300, and so I called Li Liang on his mobile.

'If I may disturb the groom for a moment, I'd like to borrow some money from you, I told him.'

A while later Li Liang arrived, slightly breathless, but carrying all manner of health food packages for my dad. When we'd completed the hospital registration formalities, Li Liang took me outside for a smoke. Fixing me with a serious look, he said he was sorry about the wine-throwing episode at the wedding yesterday. He'd like to apologise on Ye Mei's behalf.

'You soft bastard, there's no need to say that,' I replied. 'We're friends, aren't we?'

Deep down though, I was afraid that this was something it would be impossible to keep hidden from him. I felt ashamed.

At university, our dormitory gang frequently discussed one question: what would we do if we discovered after marriage that our wives weren't virgins?

Bighead Wang was the most militant. He said that second-hand goods were only fit to be used once. After that they should be thrown out. But I was sceptical. At the time of their marriage Wang's wife, whose name was Zhang Lan Lan, had well-developed breasts and an air of experience. However, Bighead had always kept quiet on the subject.

For his part, Li Liang said he didn't care about a woman's hymen. Even if she comes from a whorehouse I can accept her, as long as she doesn't mess around after marriage.

They asked me for my opinion, but my brain seized up. 'You farts, let me sleep,' I said and snapped off the light. Lying under the sheets I felt wronged, thinking about Zhao Yue's background and sensing I'd suffered a big loss.

I sensed that Li Liang was hard on the outside but vulnerable inside. Even though he said he wouldn't care, I believed he definitely would. When he was dating Mount Tai, he went crazy when Mount Tai's ex-boyfriend called her. On hearing his voice her eyes had started to well with tears. Li Liang told me about it outside the laundry one day and his expression was unusually savage. My impression was that if Li Liang had martial arts skills, that guy would definitely have been bleeding from every orifice.

I felt terrible about what had happened in Leshan.
Thinking about it made me start to hate myself a little. The
restaurant-owner's wife I'd screwed a few times once told
me, 'Your brain answers to your dick.' She had me about
right. Once Ye Mei removed her pants, I didn't think twice
about her being Li Liang's fiancée. I'd just gazed longingly
at her snowy white soft body.

After his operation Father felt low. We took it in turns to
keep him company at the hospital, and the May holiday
slipped by without us realising. The old man didn't have
much to say to me, but I knew that in his reticent smile was
a strength I could rely on

One night as I was leaving the hospital, I saw Zhou Yan
from work walk past with a handsome guy on her arm.
They were chatting away happily. I called her name and
she turned her head and asked coldly what was up. I said
I was sorry for what had happened and that it hadn't been
deliberate. The handsome guy instantly became alert, like
a donkey that's been flogged.

Zhou Yan really seemed to hate me now. 'It doesn't matter whether it was intentional or not,' she said. 'Anyway, I
now know what a dickhead you are.' And she walked away.

I ran after her. 'Zhou Yan, Zhou Yan, let me explain.'

Her donkey boyfriend turned and shoved me, swearing
at me furiously: 'Fuck you, what do you want?'

Angry, I stopped chasing them. I felt a real sense of loss
and thought, if this had happened a few years ago, I would

have bashed the crap out of him. I was more mature now!

Ah, back in the old days, I was pretty hard. There was a guy in our courtyard called Lang Four, and he was the best fighter around. During my second-grade year he and two other guys beat this vegetable stall vendor to death and then fled to the north-east. When he came back three years later his infamy spread even further. It was said that he'd slept with every attractive girl in our neighbourhood. My adolescent self admired him immensely. I frequently hung out with him at his home or on the street, feeling very tough.

Once, two hooligans were hassling some female class-mates on the way to school. When I tried to defend the girls I found the hooligans were stronger than me so I gave Fourth Brother a call.

'Brother, there are some guys bullying me,' I told him.

Fourth Brother turned up with a kitchen knife. As soon as I saw him my courage was boosted and, with a single punch, I hit one of the thugs in the face and drew blood. This story was recounted admiringly by my classmates for some time. From my point of view it didn't work out so well though, as one of the girls I'd saved, the one I'd liked, became yet another of Fourth Brother's conquests. My heart was broken for the first time the day I went over to his room after class and saw her there.

Fourth Brother made amends, however, by helping to arrange a 'coming of age' ceremony for me at the end of my second year at high school. He called Pang Yuyan over and said, 'Little Rabbit is still a boy. Today you can help him become a man.'

Pang Yuyan immediately took off her pants. A little while later I came out of the room highly embarrassed and told Fourth Brother, 'Fuck her, Pang Yuyan has BO.'

Today, Lang Four has an internet café on Yinsi Street and a very ugly wife. One day when I dropped by he said, 'You can go online. I won't charge you.'

I'd hardly sat down when his wife started making a fuss about it. Her squawking disturbed the whole room. Lang Four looked embarrassed, so I smiled at him and left quickly. I spent a while looking at the dazzling lights of New Times Square, where, fourteen years before, there was a vegetable market where this honest and straightforward small-business owner had killed a man.

CHAPTER FOURTEEN

Our company always insisted that 'virtue resides at the top'. You could be an ass, but so long as you didn't steal or have a messy sex life you had your chance of becoming a manager. Fatty Dong spouted this bull-shit at every opportunity. His implication was that because he had become a boss he was highly virtuous. Shortly before the 1 May holiday, he convened a big company meeting, the whole purpose of which was to attack me.

Fatty Dong gave me a righteous look and said, 'If a person lacks responsibility towards his family, how can we hope he will act responsibly at work?'

I was equally rude. Taking his cue, I said I agreed with General Manager Dong's view and called for consistency. 'Colleagues should show responsibility for their families and for the company, and not have different rules for those at the top and those lower down.'

Liu Three looked ready to chip in, but after a savage glare from me he shut up and sat down again in a hurry.

At work, I already had a reputation for womanising. Once again I had Fatty Dong to thank for this. Last year the deputy chair of the board had come to Chengdu to inspect us. He'd sought me out and warned me to pay close attention to my lifestyle.

'Be a good, responsible man,' he said.

I was annoyed. I haven't seduced your wife or daughter, I thought. What gossip have you heard?

Naturally it was Fatty Dong who'd prescribed me this bitter medicine. I gave up any thoughts of becoming general manager. My only hope was to get through the next two years without rocking the boat, resolve my debt problem, and then find an opportunity to quit. My ideal would be to open a car repair place. Get Li Liang to invest, and then lure master mechanic Li to join me. I was sure we'd make money. Thinking about it made me sad though, because when I was younger my aspirations were much grander. I'd wanted to be an expert at something, or else a heroic gangster. Now the extent of my ambitions was to be some kind of small boss. The water level of my life was sinking lower and lower, and it seemed nothing would be as great as I'd dreamed it would.

Fatty Dong's composure was impressive. Whether conducting meetings, talking to colleagues, or processing documents, there was barely a chink. I admired his self-control. When the pre-holiday meeting broke up, however, he tilted his head and watched me for ages, giving me the creeps. This guy wasn't stupid; he'd work out who'd set him up.

I couldn't see any definite sign that trouble was coming, but I was still quick to set my plans in motion. I'd already faxed Head Office the report about him going whoring and leaping out the window. Fatty Dong, stripped of his outer packaging, was more degenerate than me. I was confident that this framer of others wouldn't be general manager for much longer. 'Virtuous people at the top'—well, he'd said it.

The first day back after the holiday I was constantly either on the telephone or signing documents. Liu Three's treachery didn't bother me. He wouldn't be able to do anything without me because I was in with all our clients.

Our longstanding Neijiang sales agent was holding on to a 4 million advance that he should have returned. Although Liu Three had been working on it for over a month he hadn't got a damn bit of it back yet. Gloomily he came to find me and confess.

'Haven't you already outgrown me?' I said. 'Why don't you tell Boss Dong? Why come to me?'

Liu was pale. He said, 'You're the sales team manager. This is your responsibility.'

I made a face and then picked up the telephone and called the sales agent. 'Screw you, Wang Yu. If you don't give back the money be careful I don't get you chopped.'

Wang Yu derided me in turn. 'You bastard, I knew you wanted money from me,' he said.

He said he'd himself recently with a young bar singer.

She was beautiful, sang sweetly and had great sexual tech-nique, especially anal. This guy was a rascal. As soon as there was any serious business at hand, he started filling the sky with nonsense.

'Shut up and give us the money,' I said.

Wang Yu stopped fooling around. 'I'll give you the first 2 million this afternoon, but you'll have to wait a few days for the rest.'

I looked at Liu Three then deliberately raised my voice. 'If I don't see all the money tomorrow, I'll turn your son into dog meat dumplings.'

I'd met a girl like Wang Yu's singer myself, at the Glasshouse bar. Her family name was Zhang, but she used the coquettish stage name Gentle Flower. Before she sang she would warble the following sentence: Gentle Flower performs a few songs for you.

Her voice was good though, and she was a natural per-former with stage presence, graceful movements and long hair. She had an air of classical beauty—refined and full of sex appeal. At one time I was going to see her nearly every day. To declare my intentions I sent her a 480 yuan-per-stem rose and an 1888 yuan bottle of Hennessy XO. My approaches had the desired effect and she let me have my way with her in the back of the company's beaten-up old Santana. Afterwards, I felt as if I'd lost something. I told Li Liang, 'Once you take off her clothes, this goddess is really just flesh.'

'You always expect too much from life,' Li Liang replied.

That day Zhou Yan didn't show up for work, so I had to supervise the car repair business myself. What with ordering new fitting machine parts right through to paying the cleaners' salaries, I signed a huge pile of papers. Zhou Yan was good at her job. In the past two years I'd rarely had to worry about the car factory. The business had grown steadily, but her salary was still only 2200 or so, just half of Liu Three's. I decided to lower disloyal Liu Three's salary and give Zhou Yan at least 3000. That day when I saw her with donkey man they seemed close, so I guessed they were doing it. To use one of Bighead's phrases, it was *'a big pile of cowshit in a vase'*. When I thought of Zhou Yan sleeping with that guy, I had this feeling like I'd lost my wallet.

Every Monday there was a meeting where the department managers had to put their heads together and develop strategy. It started at 4 pm. I checked my watch constantly, wishing that Fatty Dong was dead. I didn't see how he could have the face now to sit up on that platform talking about his dog shit morals. But at the meeting, Boss Dong made a brilliant tactical move. He didn't talk about professional ethics; he didn't talk about loyalty. Instead, when he opened his mouth, he criticised himself. He said he'd let himself down, disappointed everyone's trust in him and caused the Sichuan branch to lose face. Because of this, he'd no wish to continue serving as general manager.

'I've already handed in my resignation to Head Office,'

he said. 'I just hope I can continue to serve the company in some lowly capacity.'

He worked himself up into an emotional state, crying actual tears, so that those who weren't familiar with the real situation felt deep sympathy for him. I smiled coldly, thinking that the guy really knew how to put on a performance. It was a tragic waste that he hadn't gone for a career in acting.

It was sheer genius. On the one hand he was admitting fault; on the other he was expressing his devotion to the company. As I studied his fat face, I was torn between exasperation and admiration. Head Office wouldn't be too hard on him, I guessed. At most they'd impose some kind of symbolic penalty.

When we first started at the company, I'd actually liked Fatty Dong a lot. A chubby guy, he seemed like one of those straightforward, good-natured types. In the first half of 1995 we often went drinking together. When he got married I gave him 200 yuan in a red envelope—a serious gift at that time. We didn't start our feud until he became head of the administration department. Back then I was still an ordinary member of the sales team. After Fatty got promoted he immediately became very grand, speaking with unbearable pomposity. Once there was a document on his desk which I idly picked up. He acted as if he'd caught a thief, and covered it up saying, 'This isn't for your eyes.' I went off in a huff, resenting his arrogance. From that time on he and I never saw eye to eye. Before long I too started to get promoted, from supervisor to manager. For a time I was actually in a position one grade higher than Fatty. Sick with jealousy, Fatty Dong badmouthed me, both openly and behind my back. I was pretty rude as well. During meetings I'd attack by innuendo: hinting at his hypocrisy, the way he had one image in public and another in private, how he played the king on stage and removed women's skirts off stage. After our first few bouts we each suffered injuries, but the fires of war continued to burn. When he became general manager, they blazed white hot.

After work I went to the hospital to see my father. My mother was supporting him as he took a walk around the ward. I admired their relationship and wondered whether, thirty years from now, Zhao Yue and I would be that close.

During the time my dad was in hospital our lives were so busy we didn't even have time to argue. There was a kind of artificial respect and politeness between us, like you have with a guest. But that telephone call I'd made to Zhao Yue's lover still cut my heart like a knife. The pain penetrated all our embraces, kisses and kind words. My senior high school physics teacher had introduced me to the meaning of 'entropy', and I thought now that all life was entropy. Everything slowly fragmented and nothing stayed perfect.

I withdrew 2000 with my card to pay back Li Liang. Actually I'd borrowed at least 10,000 or 20,000 from him at the mahjong table and so paying back this much was just a gesture. However, I was aware that at some critical time in the future, Li Liang might be the only person who could lend me money.

Li Liang was playing mahjong again. Ye Mei sat opposite, and on either side of him were two men I didn't know. The scene was exactly the same as that time the month before when I'd gone round. Sometimes life demonstrated its bittersweet nature by taking you full circle. It was as if the last month had been a dream. The CD player was still playing 'Scarborough Fair'. This time, however, Li Liang was cleaning up at the table.

Ye Mei's face slowly reddened. I couldn't tell whether Li Liang noticed.

When I got out the money for Li Liang, he gave me a kick and said, 'That was a gift to your folks.'

Embarrassed, I put the money back in my pocket. Ye Mei gave me a mean look, and I blushed, wishing I could find a crack in the earth to swallow me up.

Li Liang asked whether I knew about what had happened to Big Brother. I asked what was up, and Li Liang covered his tiles and looked at me, saying slowly, 'Big Brother was murdered two days ago, in Shenyang. Some young thug.'

I just gaped at him.

Our former classmate Big Brother's real name was Tong Qinwei. He was one metre eighty-five, a true north-easterner. After graduation he went back to his hometown but things didn't go so well for him there. First he was fired from his job, then he got divorced, and he seemed to lose

his way. In 1999 he visited us in Chengdu. As soon as he
arrived he started to complain about life, his face full of felt
injustice. In the four years since we'd last seen him he'd got
some white hairs and it was painful to look at him. When
he left, Li Liang, Bighead and I pooled together to give him
10,000 yuan. Big Brother was so moved that his lip started
to tremble. Later though, I heard that he went everywhere
looking for old classmates to borrow money from. When he
got the money, he spent it on women. Chen Chao called
especially to warn me: 'For god's sake, don't give him any
money. He's a completely different person these days.'

Big Brother was acknowledged by our crowd to be the
one who most valued personal loyalty. If there was ever any
fighting to be done, you only had to mention it to him and
he'd pile in to protect you. Apart from drinking, his favourite pastime was girls. Most of Chen Chao's sex knowledge
had been acquired from Big Brother.

One day Li Liang was reading aloud Shi Ting's poem
'Goddess Peak': *The view from a mountain peak for 1000
years can't compare to crying on a lover's shoulder for one
night.*

Big Brother had shaken his head and muttered darkly,
'No good. If it were me, I'd change it to 'Jerking off for
one thousand years can't compare to one night of fucking.'
From then on we called him the 'Fucking Monk'.

Li Liang sighed. 'Now I'm really starting to believe in
fate,' he said. 'I never thought Big Brother would end this
way.'

I didn't say anything, but I was remembering Big Brother

carting me crazily around the campus on a pushbike, telling me: 'If only a girl would sleep with me, I could devote my whole life to her.'

Eight years later, he was dust.

This thought greatly depressed me. After dinner, Zhao Yue asked me to clean the plates but I pretended not to hear. Zhao Yue was pissed off and went to clean the plates herself.

When I heard the sound of something breaking I snapped, 'If you don't want to clean them, just leave them. You don't need to show your bad mood at every opportunity.'

Zhao Yue laughed frostily. 'Who's in a bad mood? From the moment I got home you've been cold and distant. If there's something you're not happy about why don't you just say so?'

'What do I have to be unhappy about?' I asked her. 'I don't have any lover calling me at three in the morning.'

CHAPTER FIFTEEN

The day Father got out of hospital was the happiest for months. I took him home in the company Santana. Mother had prepared a table full of food, and we opened a bottle of bamboo leaf wine that we'd saved for over ten years. My brother-in-law had obtained two cartons of Zhonghua cigarettes as a bribe from a visiting work unit, and he presented one as a gift to his father-in-law. The other he gave to me, his wife's younger brother. Meanwhile, my six-year-old nephew was running wild in the kitchen. It was said that the kid already had a girlfriend at kindergarten, and that his talents in this area exceeded mine. My sister and Zhao Yue were also in the kitchen, killing a fish. I couldn't hear what they were talking about.

Over dinner, my sister's husband talked about a recent suicide case in the suburbs. A laid-off worker called Lou,

who ran a small stall in the night market, suffered a random
city inspection. Some of his basins and jars were confiscated. Lou and a few of the other traders protested. Hoping
to get their goods back, they followed the city inspector's
car a couple of kilometres, but without any success. In a
sudden fury Lou threw stones and bricks at the official's
car. What they hadn't foreseen was that while the official
escaped unscathed, a young man passing by received a fatal
blow. After running home, the more Lou thought about the
situation the more frightened he became. He and his wife
cried on each other's shoulders and he said, 'Let's end it
all.' His wife agreed there was really no point in living and
the two tearfully fed their child rat poison, then closed the
windows and turned on the gas. The whole family died.

This story made everyone hugely depressed. My brother-
in-law added melodramatically: 'These are dark times. No
one can predict what tomorrow will bring. Everything is
false; only money is real.'

As soon as he mentioned money, I felt queasy. Yesterday the accountant had printed out my statement. When
I took a look at it, my head started spinning. There was
a total debt of 280,400 against my name. Most of it was
business loans: borrowing 10,000 and returning 6000,
with the remainder accumulating as debt. The accountant had hinted that there was a big audit coming up next
month, and that if I didn't return the money by then I'd
suffer disciplinary action. When I heard this, I broke out in
a sweat. I began to wonder whether the accountant could
have got the numbers wrong. I went over it again and again

in my mind, but the more I tried to work it out the more confused I became. I couldn't remember how I'd spent all that money. However, I guessed that if I hadn't lost it at the mahjong table, I'd spent it on women. Bighead often said that I only went to work for the sake of the lower half of my body.

After his recent misfortune, Fatty Dong was keeping a low profile. Each day he sat quietly in the office, and when walking he no longer deliberately thrust out his stomach. Head Office hadn't made a decision yet on how to handle the prostitute issue. This was typical of that group of rice buckets. No matter how pressing the issue, they still had to have a meeting and discuss all the permutations with frightening inefficiency. Last year the sales department applied for a new computer with a price tag of less than 5000 yuan. I waited for over two months while the report bounced from desk to desk, eventually collecting around fifteen signatures. I thought that if Fatty Dong's brothel liaison had resulted in a child, the decision on how to deal with him would have taken forever.

Recently, the jerk seemed to have become friendlier. There was some bowing and scraping, and he even offered me cigarettes a few times. The previous Saturday when I'd gone in to prepare our advance orders for the month, I met him in the lift. He said that once again he'd recommended me to be general manager.

'Even though we don't get on that well, I still admire your ability,' he told me.

I couldn't help feeling slightly flattered, although I

didn't know whether he was lying.

It would be heaven if I did get to be general manager. At our current volume of sales, the position would come with a salary of around 300,000 a year. Then there was a car, and expenses for just about anything. The company also offered interest-free loans to help with buying a house. Fatty Dong had borrowed 150,000 yuan, saying it was for a house but actually using it to invest in stocks. Apart from the twice-yearly review, Head Office didn't interfere in branch office operations. If you added together the official salary and the hidden rewards, in three years the general manager could easily clear more than 1 million yuan. It was a cushy number. Lots of our competitors were ex-senior executives from our company. After getting turfed out, Boss Sun had started a company in Tianjin and, apparently, business was sweet. My biggest problem was that sometimes I was careless in both words and deeds. My mouth had no gate—it let anything out—and sometimes I even hit the table in front of my superiors. All this gave Head Office the impression that I was immature, a loose cannon. But after Fatty Dong's comments, I wondered whether I should take the initiative and put myself forward for the general manager position. Perhaps I should write Head Office a report on my work..

I thought I'd ask for my father's advice. After reflecting on his many years at the same work unit, he offered the following insight. To be a top official didn't require outstanding achievements, but just three things: glibness, an effective pen and the ability to boast. Once you reached a certain level you didn't even need all these skills your-self—you had assistants and secretaries to help you. At least I had the extra advantage of being able to write magnifi-cent reports full of incisive words and enthusiasm. My pen could turn a broken temple into an imperial palace.

When I got home and mentioned the possible promotion to Zhao Yue, she began to dance with excitement. She said that if it happened then she would finally 'eat' me with her mouth. I wondered gloomily who she would be eating; me or a general manager?

My comment the other day about her lover had left Zhao Yue speechless. It had taken her ages to collect her-self. Then she'd coughed and said I was crazy.

'Who saw me make a phone call at three in the morn-ing?' she demanded.

I said the telephone number. She looked blank and said that she'd never dialled that number. She had no memory of it.

'You're wrong about that,' I said bitterly.'

Jumping to her feet, she said that I was deliberately try-ing to spoil things between us.

Furious, I produced the pile of telephone bills from my bag. Smacking them down on the sofa, I said, 'Look for yourself.'

Zhao Yue looked through the bills. Gradually her face reddened.

'I remember now,' she said slowly. 'That's one of our

department's external supervisors. He was writing a report at that time so he often called for my input.'

I stared at her, feeling pained, thinking how we'd grown apart. There was really nothing more to say.

In the film *Ashes of Time*, the actress Lin Qing Xia had the following line: *If there comes a day when I can't bear to ask you, you must have cheated on me.* This had long been one of Zhao Yue's favourite phrases. When passions were high, she often quoted it to me. Before, when she'd repeated the line, I'd embraced her, believing her to be loving and honest. But now I'd realised that was a false impression. Once the toilet has been flushed, it is clean and fresh enough to wash your feet in; it seemed my Zhao Yue wasn't as pure as I'd thought.

Zhao Yue and I hadn't bothered with a big wedding; we'd just treated a few close friends to a meal. Bighead, Li Liang and Chen Chao, who'd made a special trip to take part in our wedding, all had fun making the traditional racket outside our bridal chamber. After our guests left, Zhao Yue waved her arms around as if she was scattering happiness. 'Fom now on, you are mine!' she declared.

I smiled and took her in my arms, I couldn't help thinking of that stirring piece of Communist party oratory: 'On this battlefield we have lost our bridle and gained a whole world'. My version: 'On this battlefield I've lost my world and gained a bridle'.

Zhao Yue was good to me for the first few years of our marriage, but I always felt that she devoted more of her attention to controlling me. She seemed to care more about my fidelity than my health. It only needed me to come home slightly late and, with a glum face, she'd ask me over and again: 'Where were you? What were you doing? Who were you with?'

At first I'd try to explain, but eventually I got fed up and started being cold and indifferent. Zhao Yue's anxiety had an impact on our crockery: every month she broke a few bowls.

For the following few days after my mention of the general manager position, Zhao Yue was extra loving. She even bought me a few Gold Lion ties. One night, on our way home after visiting my elder sister and husband, we passed the KaKa Bar and she suggested going in. 'It's been ages since we had a dance,' she said.

Zhao Yue was a hot dancer. One time our university organised a fraternity dance competition, and Zhao Yue and a boy from her class won second prize, which made me jealous for days. When it came to dancing I only had a few basic moves. Zhao Yue said that my dancing looked like I had a bad case of piles. As a result, I rarely set foot in discos. But I didn't have any problem with going to bars. Drinking was the best way for people to forget their worries.

Under the dim lights, Zhao Yue was a lithe and graceful dancing queen. Her long hair flew and her eyes glowed like precious stones. Two young guys nearby couldn't take their eyes off her. When the disco really got pumped up, Zhao Yue's moves became even more alluring. She danced alone, pulsating to the music. Onlookers applauded her loudly, fanning my vanity so that I couldn't resist blowing her a kiss. Zhao Yue flashed me a glance as she twisted and turned.

At that moment, I realised that her mobile was ringing, and setting down my glass, I groped through the many pockets of her handbag before finding the phone. The music reached a crescendo; the bar was sparkling with disco lights. I held the phone up to the lights, but I already knew which number it would be.

CHAPTER SIXTEEN

If cities were people, Chengdu would be a happy drifter with a complete lack of ambition. Chengdu's soft dialect melts your ear. It's said that it can make a person's anger dissolve instantly. Chengdu people are famous idlers. Feet stretched out in a rattan chair with a glass of tea, or at the mahjong table, their lives are a fleeting dusk. When you visit famous historical spots such as Qing Yang Palace, Wu Hou Temple or Du Fu's cottage, you get the sense that throughout history there have been too many people happy to spend 5 yuan to sit around all day with a glass of tea. Their lives were as weak and flavourless as tea leaves that have been reused several times.

That weekend, the gang gathered at Du Fu's cottage to play mahjong—Bighead Wang, Li Liang and the rest. Li Liang and Ye Mei started fighting over some tiles. Ye Mei's pale face went red, Li Liang's goblin face was white. Both were puffed up with rage.

Bighead and I tried to smooth things over.

'You are still on your honeymoon,' I said. 'Why fall out over some tiles? Is there anything that can't be solved by talking?'

Bighead Wang said solemnly, 'If you like, we'll get out of the way so you two can release some heat.'

I exploded with laughter and Zhao Yue started snorting.

Ye Mei glowered at Bighead and said, 'So petty. What kind of man are you?'

Li Liang's eyes bulged as if he was possessed by a toad spirit. I quickly dragged him away, telling Ye Mei to wrap it up. Ye Mei gave me a hostile look but kept silent.

After that we abandoned mahjong and quietly drank tea. Secretly I was thinking it was bad luck that the game had been abandoned just when Li Liang owed me 200 yuan. We stuck it out until dinner time, and then Li Liang drove us to the China Hotel where the boss was all smiles.

'Master Li, we haven't seen you for a long time,' he said. 'The five-grain wine you saved here last time will soon be going bad.'

Bighead said, 'Rich people are different. They wear expensive clothes, and everywhere they go people kiss their arses.'

The boss clapped his hands and laughed.

During the meal, Bighead told a few dirty stories. These restored my appetite and, lowering my head, I launched an assault on the salmon. Bighead was talking up a storm but then suddenly I realised he'd stopped. Reluctantly lifting my head, I saw that Li Liang and Ye Mei were eyeballing each other like two cocks in a fight. If they weren't sitting on opposite sides of the table they'd already have started snapping at each other. I held my hand in front of Li Liang's eyes to block their glares and sighed inwardly, Aiya, all lovers are enemies from a past life.

After eating we all went our separate ways. Bighead and his wife said they had to look at a house; this decadent couple now found their own place too small. Li Liang took Ye Mei home, where I presumed their war was about to resume. I had no idea who would come off worst. Zhao Yue hinted that she wanted me to go shopping with her, but I refused, saying I had to go the office to write a report.

There were days when we didn't argue, but even then it felt as if we'd become like strangers. To judge by appearances though, we were more in love than ever. When we left home, we looked at each other and smiled. Coming back at night, we smiled and looked at each other. Whenever we were going to be late home for some reason or other, we'd call the other to check that was OK.

Zhou Weidong found this strange behaviour. 'Chen, bro, when did you become a new man?' he asked me.

I smiled mirthlessly. I'd never brought up the subject of the telephone call that night at the disco with Zhao Yue. When we got home, I'd gone into the bathroom to cool down and then heard her speaking softly on the telephone outside. I pressed my ear against the door and listened for ages but was unable to hear exactly what she was saying. When I came out, Zhao Yue put on a fake smile. From that point on, I started to take note of her whereabouts. Secretly I went through her handbag, even inspected her discarded panties. I didn't know what I thought I'd find, or what I'd do if I did find anything. Because of that I hated myself a little; I wasn't a real man.

I didn't know if it was because of my bad detective work or because Zhao Yue was brilliant at deception, but I didn't discover anything suspicious. Of course, just because I didn't find anything didn't mean that nothing had happened. I detected a certain something in the look of slight resistance on Zhao Yue's face as we made love, and her lost expression afterwards. Three months before, when Zhao Yue had told me she had a lover, I'd been sure that she was lying. Since she was now denying everything, that meant she'd gone over to the dark side. Li Liang said I was too fond of perverse logic, but perverse logic was a weapon, I thought with a cold smile.

My report quickly reached seven or eight thousand words. First I told the story of how a rank-and-file salesman became a manager. This was taking a leaf out of Bighead Wang's book. Last year at the security bureau's public speaking competition he'd won first prize with his address, 'From plain cop to station chief'. After his win he'd been unbearably smug, boasting incessantly to me and Li Liang. Only after we changed 'plain cop' to 'plain cock' did he shut up.

Once I'd set the scene, I went on to list all my hard work that year. The report was a thorough blend of direct description and subtlety. It had a summary, it had action points, it had emotion. It even had lyrical passages. Reading it over, I felt sure it would hit the spot for that bunch of rice heads at Head Office. After faxing it through, I leaned back in my chair and fantasised about general manager Chen Zhong: driving a Honda with a babe at my side, wallet stuffed full of notes.

Thinking about girls, I suddenly remembered a babe I'd met once when I was drinking tea in Yulin South Road internet café. She was called Niu something or other. She was tall and slender with substantial firm breasts, a round face and an attractive smile. That day she'd acted hot for me, giving me plenty of flirtatious glances. Finally she'd left me her telephone number, saying, 'If you have time, let's do something.'

After searching my desk drawers for ages, I actually found her number. For a moment my heart was savage with joy. I dialled and through a racket on the other end of the line heard some man asking me who I was looking for. I said I wanted to find little Niu. He said, 'What little cow?[15] Wrong number!'

I didn't give up, simply dialled the number again. This time as soon as the guy heard my voice he started to curse. 'Screw you, didn't I say you've dialled the wrong number!' He slammed down the receiver.

My fury knew no bounds. I dialled the number once again, and as soon as the other person picked up I let loose a volley of curses. 'Screw your mother, screw your sister. Screw your wife!'

I left the building still aggrieved, glaring at people in the street as though they owed me money. I went into the car park and looked all around but couldn't find the Santana. Of course it had to be that prick Liu Three who'd taken it. I dialled his cell phone. This was the first time we'd had any kind of private contact in more than a month.

'What's up?' Liu Three answered.

'I need the car. Please return it immediately.'

He said that his sister was moving house and they were using the car to transport a few things.

'There's nothing I can do about that,' I said. 'I need to take a client to the repair centre.'

Very resentfully, Liu Three returned the car. I just stood there impassively, and when he shut the car door he turned and left without a word. I glared at his back, thinking, You cheeky sod. How dare you show your bad temper in front of your superior?

Liu Three's salary was hardly any less than mine; each month he got more than 4000 basic and then commissions on top. In a good month it could exceed 10,000. But the guy was incredibly tight. Whenever we went out to eat, he never offered to pay. Zhou Weidong called him 'iron wallet'. Those two had a relationship which was a little like mine and Fatty Dong's in the early days. They were secretly

at war, and whenever they had an opportunity they attacked
each other. I often had to calm them down, blaming both
sides without prejudice so they didn't dare to take their
quarrel too far. Zhou Weidong's temperament was rather
like mine. He was always spending money, and when he
saw a pretty girl he drooled. If it wasn't for his unfortunate
compulsion to dwell on my flaws, he'd probably have risen
faster than Liu Three.

A couple of days before, I'd successfully annoyed Liu
Three by finding a pretext to deduct 600 yuan from his
salary. Fatty Dong had tried to intervene to no avail. Apparently Liu Three was beside himself.

As I thought about company stuff, I found myself
missing Zhou Yan a little. After the May holidays she'd
asked for a few days' sick leave. Not long after that, she'd
resigned. I spent ages trying to talk her round, construct-
ing an argument that roamed from China's opening up,
to the WTO, to the Gulf War—a panoramic sweep of
national and international affairs. Although I talked my
arse off, I still couldn't get her to stay. She sat in my office
for a while, her big eyes red. By the look of things she
felt sad about leaving. As for me, my heart was pound-
ing. We chatted about a lot of things. She explained about
her and Donkey's relationship, leading me to understand
that they'd slept together many times secretly. I burned
with jealousy. Finally Zhou Yan warned me that I should
beware.

'I can't say that you're a good person but you're not a
completely terrible person either,' she said. 'You've still got

a bit of confused goodness in you, and I'm afraid that you'll be the one to suffer in the end.'

I drove along the road by the university. A few smoking kebab stands stood on either side, and groups of grungy students with clean, fresh faces wandered up and down. Today's university students were more modern than my generation. It was said that computer illiterates and virgins were both endangered species. After midnight, there were porn films shown in a screening room outside the campus gates. This immature but formidable generation of young people watched and aspired to emulate. When Bighead was transferred to that district, he'd once made a surprise inspection of the screening room and caught a couple 'on the job'. When he shone his torch on them, the guy blasted him: 'What are you looking at? I've got a ticket!'

Today I was in the mood for love. After all, at that moment I couldn't say whose arms Zhao Yue was lying in. Boss Sun had a saying: 'Human life is all about two things, food and sex.' This, at least, he had seen clearly. I lit up a cigarette and thought that in this life you shouldn't torture yourself. The dissolute will take advantage of the young. If you could be happy for a while, then settle for that.

There was a female student just ahead of me: average height with a slender waist and full buttocks. From behind she was really something. I drove slowly past, stuck my head out and asked, 'Beauty, do you want to come to a bar?'

She gave me a contemptful look. 'Dickhead!'

Despite driving a full circuit, I couldn't see any more girls to my liking. The hot ones were all with boyfriends. I got out of the car and bought a bottle of Blue Sword beer and a few beef kebabs. While eating I continued to look up and down the street, having decided to kill a bit of time. When I saw a girl I liked, I'd go for the direct approach, asking her to go for a drink. My basic advantage in chasing girls was that I had a thick skin in the face of setbacks. I wasn't ugly, I wore smart clothes and shoes, and drove a car, so I seemed glamorous to these green college students. As long as I wasn't afraid of failure then I was sure to enjoy success.

In half an hour I made four approaches, experienced four rejections, and got called 'mental' once. At last one girl didn't refuse outright, but said she had something else on, so it would have to be another night. All the while the kebab vendor stared at me knowingly.

Still feeling restless, I was deliberating whether to stick it out or go to a KTV bar and pick a working girl. Just then, Li Liang called.

'Can you talk now?' he said in a solemn tone.

'Go ahead, what's up?'

'Help me to find a prostitute,' he ordered.

'You fuck-up, you've must have eaten something bad,' I said. 'You never use prostitutes. And what if Ye Mei finds out? She'll kill me too.'

'Are you coming or not?' he cut in. 'If not, I'll ask someone else.'

'OK, OK, I'll come. But if you're doing this because

you're angry with Ye Mei, I advise you to think about it. What about loyalty?'

He was silent a moment, then said in a loud, pointed voice: 'Who should I be loyal to?'

CHAPTER SEVENTEEN

Before Yei Mei, Li Liang hadn't had a girlfriend since graduation. Sometimes he'd accompany me to a nightclub but he always sat there like a stiff. At most he might put an arm around the hostess's shoulder. Back in 1999 he hadn't bought his Audi yet. He'd only just got his licence and he was obsessed with driving. As soon as the weekend came, we'd go for a spin. One day we drove together to Mianyang, and stopped at Jianmei Peace and Happiness City. This place was one of my occasional refuges. It was a real palace, and at its peak there could be more than a hundred girls sitting around in the large reception area.

The central sofa spilled over with low-cut cleavages, short skirts and fragrant flesh—a delectable array of young bodies to cater for society's omnipresent lust. I chose a tall and generously proportioned girl for Li Liang, then pushed him to take her to a room. He was reluctant, and so I threatened him: If you pretend to be so virtuous, I won't take you out with me in future. With a pained look he entered the room.

I deliberated for a long time before choosing a girl whose face was a little like Zhou Yan's. After some banter, we embraced and went upstairs. My girl was extremely professional, never giving the impression that she was rushing things. From start to finish she was most obliging. Once we'd done the business I left satisfied, then I noticed that Li Liang's door was still closed. I thought admiringly that although the guy looked feeble he was actually a long-distance runner.

After another half an hour, by which time I'd drunk quite a lot of beer, the two of them came downstairs. Something made me suspicious and when I got the chance I asked the girl, 'Is my friend depraved?'

She made a face and said that Li Liang hadn't even taken off his shoes. Instead, his hands clasped behind his back, he'd given her a sincere lecture: 'You're young, you could do anything. Do you really have to do this?'

I laughed. Later though, I felt bad for Li Liang. He was just too uptight.

Although I'd known Li Liang for ten years, I didn't really understand him. What pain was there in Li Liang's world? What happiness? I hadn't a clue.

At our graduation dinner he drank seven bottles of beer and fell into a stupor. Bighead and I helped him back to the dormitory. Halfway there he suddenly struggled free, and threw himself on to the ground. Wrapping his arms round a street lamp, he cried a mixture of snot and tears. No matter how hard we pulled at him he wouldn't let go of the lamp. Later, he told us that his mother had died young and that he'd gone to primary school dressed in ragged clothes. Li Liang generally looked very uncomfortable whenever we asked him about the past. His face would flush red and his veins bulge. Very scary. His father had been to Chengdu a few times, but Li Liang was always very cool towards him, his expression one of distant weariness.

Chengdu at night always looked gentle and soft. The colourful lanterns gave it a warm glow, and from all around came sounds of laughter and song. But I knew that for all its lustre the city was slowly rotting. A tide of lust and greed surged from every corner, bubbling away, giving off a hot odour, like a stream of piss corroding every tile and every soul. Just like that poet Li Liang said:

Last night God died
Heaven is crawling with maggots and snakes

At that moment, the poet was sat at my side smoking endless cigarettes. His face was as gloomy as an eggplant.

I sometimes wondered whether Li Liang had some sexual problem. During our university years our method of washing outselves was to empty a basin of cold water over our heads, even in the depths of winter. As the water flowed down our bodies we'd wail insanely. Girls going past the shower room during this scene would scream and jump. In our bored state we often evaluated each other's dicks: whose was long? whose thick? whose foreskin the longest? But Li Liang always modestly wore underpants. Once Wang Jian from the next-door dorm made a grab for them. Li Liang was incensed and wanted to get a knife to stab Wang Jian. Bighead and I thought he was making a fuss about nothing. Now, though, I reflected that the secret of Li Liang's happiness and sadness in this life was perhaps concealed in that pair of wet pants.

Just as I'd expected, as soon as Li Liang and his wife were out of our sight that day they'd escalated their crazy argument. Li Liang had driven the car straight ahead in a fury, his foot pressed hard on the accelerator. They nearly had a collision at Nine-Eyes Bridge, and at some point there must have been some kind of fight because he had a plaster on his right hand. According to Li Liang's story, Ye Mei had got out of the car, called some guy and then jumped straight into a taxi. As she left, she'd spat out some words that made Li Liang furious: 'Fuck you. Tomorrow I'll divorce you!'

Li Liang said he'd never realised she was such a coarse woman. My long sigh expressed my thought that I'd discovered this early on.

We were on our way to Guanghani Caesar Hotel, the Chengdu suburbs' most famous high-class pleasure area. I took my richest clients there, and Li Liang was also—how should I put it—one of the moneyed classes. There was no way he'd ever eat at a street stall like I still did. After passing Green Dragon Square, I called Zhao Yue. I said that something was up with Li Liang and I needed to keep him company and so would be late home. Zhao Yue didn't say anything. I hung up and gave Li Liang a look. Actually, life was pretty much the same thing, whether you were clean and honest or filthy and corrupt, I thought.

The mamasan at the Kaisa Hotel was called Yao Ping, a woman in her thirties and a legend. Her figure and appearance were more high class and beautiful than any young Hong Kong or European woman. Ten years ago, half the city's young men were willing to fight for her. On seeing me, Yao Ping presented me with a smile like a bunch of flowers.

'You've forgotten about me. You haven't been here for so long.'

'That's impossible,' I said honestly. 'I'll never forget you.'

The last time that I'd come here with Zhao Dajiang and his gang, I'd looked at a lot of girls but couldn't find one to satisfy me. I sat there grumbling. Finally Yao Ping said, 'I'll go with you,' and then led me to her room andgave a breathtaking display of her skills. Afterwards she wouldn't accept any money. She said that she was old and didn't merit payment and that I should think of it as a gift of friendship. I understood that she was being modest because her words radiated a fierce self respect. I'd heard that there a nmayor from some city in Guangdong province once asked for her. She refused him out of hand and didn't give him any face.

I embraced her luscious body and deliberately kept

my gaze averted from the forest of beautiful girls. 'Today I'm not playing,' I said. 'You just need to give my younger brother a good time.'

She gracefully extended her hand to Li Liang. 'Apart from me, you are free to choose any of the girls,' she said.

Li Liang said, 'I'm not interested in any of them, only you.'

'I'm so old, I'd be embarrassed to go to bed with you. You should choose someone fresh and tender.'

Li Liang's face set. 'I'll pay 2000.'

'It's not about money,' she said. 'I don't do that any more.'

Li Liang continued to increase his bid: 'Five thousand. No, 10,000.'

She refused, still smilingly.

'Fifteen thousand.'

Now the girls gathered around and looked at Li Liang with deep respect. Yao Ping's smile froze. She gave me an appalled glance. I grabbed Li Liang, but he struggled free and, as if in a trance, raised his offer one more time.

'Twenty thousand.'

Yao Ping's face had turned white. It seemed like a whole minute went past before I heard her say, 'Listen, I know you have money, but you don't need to show it off in front of us poor working girls. I should throw you out, but today I'll give Chen Zhong face. If you want to have a good time just choose one. If you don't want to, then go.'

'Sister Yao, don't be angry,' I said quickly. 'He's naive. Don't take it to heart.'

I'd barely finished when Li Liang sprang and threw a savage punch at my head.

'Screw you!' he shouted. 'How come you never said I was naive that time you fucked my wife!'

Instantly, I was struck dumb. It was as if I'd been hit by lightning.

Li Liang and I had known each other for ten years and in all that time we'd only argued twice. Once was over a game of chess. I had thrashed him four or five games in a row and was gloatingly pleased with myself. Li Liang's whole face was red and he asked if I had the guts to play another game. After only a few moves he was mugged again by my rook. I laughingly suggested: 'I'll give you a knight, how about it?'

He threw the pieces to the ground, stormed off, and didn't speak to me for two or three days.

The second fight was more serious—it was that time when I climbed onto his bunk to get a cigarette and he pushed me off. Caught unawares, I'd fallen heavily to the ground, nearly breaking my leg. When I'd picked myself up, I said angrily, 'What's your problem? I was just after your cigarettes.'

He was furious too. 'Who do you think you are?' he yelled. 'Don't you know the first thing about manners? How did I know whether you wanted to get a cigarette or to steal something?'

My lungs felt they might explode. I grabbed a stool and went for him, but Bighead and Big Brother blocked me in time. Li Liang and I hardly spoke to each other for a month after that. When we returned after the summer holiday though, he gave me a box of Red Five cigarettes, which finally took the heat out of things.

I was trembling from head to foot. Yao Ping clearly thought I was angry and waved to summon several young men. Indicating Li Liang, she said, 'Him!'

They made for Li Liang. I gulped and stood in front of him, saying, 'Sister, please don't beat him up. Today we've given you lots of trouble. I will come back another day to make an apology.'

I turned around and tried to tug Li Liang away, but he was rooted there like a stake in the ground. His face was still dark with anger.

'Don't make a scene here,' I said quietly. 'We'll only offend them. If you want to hit me let's go outside.'

He kicked me in the balls and left without saying anything, his eyes red. I dropped to the ground in a cold sweat, clutching my stomach. Yao Ping bent down and asked if I was OK. I was too embarrassed and in too much pain to do anything but groan.

'Do you want us to get him?' she asked me.

Emphatically I shook my head. 'Let him go,' I croaked. 'Don't hurt him.'

I was wretched. Tears welled in my eyes.

Yao Ping took me into a room. 'Get your pants off,' she said.

My spirit had been crushed. Like a drowning man clutching at straws, I burrowed my face into her soft belly. I thought that ten years of friendship was irreversibly over.

Yao Ping massaged my head. 'You rest here tonight. I'll spend some time with you again later.'

CHAPTER EIGHTEEN

Chengdu in June was bursting with life. The flowers were out, the markets awash with watermelons, and a scent of jasmine pervaded the air. After nightfall you'd see some people in the crowd laughing and others crying. Life was like a lavish banquet in a graveyard, with death fluttering smilingly around us. When the last traces of youth were gone, who remembered those vanished days of tenderness and pain?

For several days, Zhao Yue had been suffering with a bad cold. Each time I suggested she buy some medicine she said she was too busy. She paid for it, because one night she had a fever of 39 degrees. I piled all the quilts in the house on top of her but she still said she felt cold. We passed an uncomfortable night and the next morning I half carried her to the hospital. Zhao Yue moaned feebly the whole way. I felt sorry for her, but scolded her for not heeding my advice. 'I told you to come earlier but you didn't listen. Now you're suffering, huh?'

She lay across my arms at a crooked angle. Her breath smelt as though she'd crawled out of a fish's stomach.

Once attached to an IV drip, Zhao Yue drifted into semi-unconsciousness, her nose quivering like a three-year-old kid's. I adjusted the drip flow rate to the lowest level and wiped her face with a tissue. She held my arms tightly, and muttered that she had a headache.

I hadn't slept at all the night before and after sitting there for a while I just couldn't keep my eyes open. Leaning against the hospital bed, I drifted off. Suddenly through my befuddled haze I heard a whisper: 'Isn't that Chen Zhong?'

I opened my eye and saw a fair, buxom woman standing outside the door, making eyes at me.

I slowly withdrew my hand from Zhao Yue's chest. She was sleeping deeply with an innocent smile on her face. Walking towards the door, I waved a greeting. The woman was the wife of the owner of the Emei Tofu Restaurant. I called her 'Tofu Queen'.

'Is that your wife?' she asked.

I pinched Tofu Queen's waist and said, 'Yes. She's more beautiful than you, right?'

She humphed, pretending to be jealous.

'Come on. You play around with eight hundred handsome guys every day,' I said, 'so don't pretend to be innocent.'

Emei Tofu Restaurant was just across the street from my office. The owner, Mr Xiao, was from Leshan. Although short, he had a head like a boulder and piercing eyes, like a kung fu master. I often entertained clients in his restaurant. His chicken cooked in tofu pudding was something I especially loved: fragrant chicken boiled inside a big bowl of fresh snow-white tofu pudding with crispy vegetables. It was unimaginably delicious. After I'd been there a few times we got to know each other and soon it was 'brother' this and 'sister-in-law' that. I even flirted with Mr Xiao's wife, and she flirted back. Mr Xiao didn't seem bothered—he still proposed toasts and served dishes as usual. His hands were like big cattail leaf fans and his eyes like iron bells.

One winter night in 1999, Li Liang and I had played mahjong till one in the morning. Li Liang had lost 7000 yuan and was despondent.

'My luck's bad today,' he said. 'Let's quit and go out for some drinks.'

I took him to Emei Tofu Restaurant, where we found the owner away and Tofu Queen about to shut up for the night. I rapped on the table and said, 'Quickly, tofu chicken, tofu fish and four bottles of beer.'

After the dishes and beer were served I asked her to join us. She sat beside me and played the finger guessing game, drank, and competed in telling dirty stories. When Li Liang went out to talk to someone on his phone, she nudged my leg with her knee and said, 'My husband's not coming back tonight.'

I felt inflamed. I waited impatiently until Li Liang finished his meal then told him, 'You go home first. I have to talk to her about something.'

He gaped at me. 'Be careful that I don't tell Zhao Yue.'

At the head of their bed was a big wedding picture. Short Mr Xiao looked earnest, glaring at me intently with his searchlight eyes.

Tofu Queen asked me now if I was free that afternoon.

'Why? You want to get fucked again?' I said. I couldn't help talking dirty when I saw her. Actually she was the same. Once she called me and said outright: 'Do you want it? If you do, then come over. He's not at home.'

The first few times I'd found this a novelty, but after a while I got fed up. How was it that this woman could think about nothing but sex? She didn't display any emotion at all. She'd take off her pants and get straight on the bed, then after we'd finished she'd give a satisfied smack of her lips. What was more, she never even gave me a discount in the restaurant.

Now she trod on my foot with her heel and said, 'Your face is spotty. You need to release some heat.'

Sneaking my head round the door I saw Zhao Yue turning over in her hospital bed. She seemed oblivious to everything. I calculated: it would take about one hour to go and come back. Most likely Zhao Yue would still be asleep when I returned. Suddenly I was feverishly excited. I grabbed the woman's hand and dragged her straight for the exit.

'This time we'll go to my place so I don't have to see your husband's ugly face,' I said.

I bought the apartment at the Youth Garden in Yulin compound last year. According to Bighead Wang: 'It was a high-end residence until you lowlife moved in.'

Zhao Yue and I had argued a lot about renovations. She was slightly unhinged the whole time the property was being done up, not combing her hair or washing her face because of her anxiety that the workers might do shoddy work or use inferior materials. She practically slept at the apartment.

'Is it really worth all this fuss?' I said. 'As long as it's OK for us to live in, that's enough.'

She went berserk and ripped some wallpaper from the wall. She asked me repeatedly: 'Who am I doing this for?'

I apologised, secretly cursing her for being insane. When the renovation was done, Zhao Yue spent several days cleaning the apartment. She knelt on the floor and wiped it tile by tile. When I finally got to see it, the whole place was completely spotless.

'You've made it so clean, I don't dare go inside,' I said. 'Why don't you carry me on your back?'

Tofu Queen was about to charge inside the apartment. I hauled her back sternly.

'Take off your shoes,' I said.

She looked at me, confused.

I thought, Zhao Yue has cleaned this apartment inch by inch. What right do you have to get it dirty?

She clung to me while taking off her shoes. Her hands were oily and her body smelt of vegetable soup. Suddenly I felt a rush of disgust. When we got to the bedroom, she embraced me and wanted to kiss. I pushed her away impatiently.

'You take a shower first,' I said.

I'd always considered Tofu Queen to be dirty. There was often dirt in the cracks of her nails. Mr Xiao loved her and bought her designer clothes — even her underwear was Calvin Klein. However, they were usually smeared with chopped scallions or smashed garlic. Once I discovered she didn't even wash her hands after going to the toilet. I was disgusted and forced her to go back and wash them. She was slightly ashamed of her low habits, and each time after that whenever we met up she'd say straightaway, I've just had a shower.

This time she was annoyed though. 'What do you mean? If you look down on me, just say so directly.'

I knew I was in the wrong. Forcing a smile, I said, 'I didn't mean that. You know my wife is sick, and so I'm a bit upset.'

She said ironically, 'I didn't realise you were a good man who cared about his wife.'

With a little wiggle of her butt, she went into the bathroom.

I stuck on a rock album, lit a cigarette and paced the room. All jittery, swinging my arms, I knocked down a picture frame on the desk. When I squatted on my heels to pick it up and set it straight, I saw Zhao Yue dressed in her white wedding dress, smiling. At the back of the picture was a line of colourfully drawn rabbits. Zhao Yue's zodiac sign was the rabbit, and she believed these rabbits would bring her safety and happiness.

Tofu Queen came out of the shower naked. Glancing around the room she said, 'Your place isn't large but it's quite clean. You must have a good wife.'

Her words pained me.

She kissed me, saying, 'I haven't seen you for a month and I really missed you.'

She had perfect skin, soft and smooth, just like the best tofu pudding at her restaurant. My fires were stoked. Fatty Dong divided women into two categories: for use and for appreciation. Every time we teased him about his wife's appearance, he insisted that she was for use. 'What do you know about it?' he'd say.

I always thought he was bragging. His wife was as flat as a bench, nothing in the front or back, and so she couldn't have been very satisfying. Women like Tofu Queen, however, were definitely designed for use. She moaned as soon as I touched her.

The telephone in the living room began ringing. I wondered who was being so inconsiderate. It made enough noise to drive anyone crazy. At first I said, 'Fuck,' and ignored it, but it continued. It was as if someone was deliberately trying to annoy me. Finally I couldn't bear it any more. I grabbed the phone and demanded fiercely, 'Who is it?' Silence. I was about to put down the phone in a fury when I heard Zhao Yue say weakly, 'Open the door. I don't have my key.'

One time during the Chinese New Year in 1998, I went to the north-east with Zhao Yue and met my parents-in-law. Zhao Yue was constantly in a bad mood during that trip. I called her Sister Dai Yu.[16] The second day of Chinese New Year, after dinner at her father's place, it started snowing heavily. Despite my advice, Zhao Yue insisted on walking home. When we reached an empty alley, she stopped and said, 'I feel very sad now. Hold me!'

I held her and whispered, 'Don't be so sad. They don't love you, but you still have me.'

Zhao Yue trembled, then put her arms around my neck and started crying. I looked up and saw that the sky was full of flying flecks of snow, just like lonely moths with nowhere to go. They fell on our shoulders in tiny flakes.

That night I felt quite moved thinking about the hardships Zhao Yue had suffered while growing up. When her parents were going through their divorce she would lock herself in her room. Like a little adult, she did housework. It must have been very painful. Zhao Yue often asked me the 'forever question' and I usually gave some perfunctory answer. That time, however, I answered with great sincerity: 'I will be sweet to you forever. Stop crying Sister Dai Yu.'

No words could begin to describe my panic. I tore through the living room, then staggered into the bedroom. Even my voice sounded different.

'Hurry up, get dressed!' I said. 'My wife is back.'

Tofu Queen leapt like an uncoiled spring and started grabbing her clothes, which were scattered everywhere. As for me, I was nearly blacking out. I was truly finished this time. After she got dressed, she helped fasten my buttons then asked if there was somewhere she could hide.

I snapped nastily, 'There's nowhere to hide.'

Zhao Yue was here. How could we hope to hide from her?

Zhao Yue's face was pale. She stared at me and slumped against the wall. When I reached out to her, she angrily pushed me away, then, gasping for breath, went into the living room. Tofu Queen was there, standing by the window with a red face. My heart beat crazily and my face and body were sweating.

Zhao Yue stood there for a while then said to the restaurant-owner's wife, 'Get out.'

Her voice was hoarse and cold with a murderous tone that made me tremble.

Tofu Queen left without a word, and closed the door very softly behind her. I heard her let out a long sigh outside. Zhao Yue stared at me fiercely, her lips quivering with anger. Realising there was nothing more to fear now things had reached this stage, I met her gaze. Her eyes gradually filled with tears and her mouth stopped trembling. She broke into terrible sobs.

'You couldn't even resist such a disgusting woman!' she cried.

CHAPTER NINETEEN

It was 15 June 2001, exactly three days before our third wedding anniversary. At breakfast, Zhao Yue said, Should we wait three more days?' She lowered her head and began to sniff.

After breakfast, I found her combing her hair before a mirror. Standing behind her, I forced a smile.

You're still beautiful,' I said. 'You don't have to worry about not getting remarried.'

Before I'd finished speaking, her eyes reddened, her hands trembled and the comb dropped to the floor.

In recent years, Zhao Yue had put on weight. Staring at her body, no longer really slim, I felt a fresh stab of pain in my heart at the thought of her words that day.

'I gave you my best years.'

My tears fell on the tie she'd just recently bought for me.

Recently, we'd done enough talking for a lifetime. Zhao Yue had asked if I still remembered our first date.

'Of course I do. You were in a purple dress, with a copy of *Marxist Philosophy* in your hands.'

She asked if I remembered how I'd spied on her while she was taking a shower.

'Yes. I was standing on a stool and you splashed water on me.'

She kept asking me, asking whether I remembered. I cried and said: 'Stop asking. Of course I still remember. Those memories are memories of our love.'

Throwing herself into my arms, she cried her heart out. 'Then why did you leave me in the hospital and have sex with another woman?'

She was the one to suggest divorce, and at first I couldn't think of anything to say. After a while though I pleaded pathetically: 'I messed up. Can't you give me one more chance?'

She cried and touched my face. 'I have no idea what it will be like when I leave you, but I'll never be able to forget what happened that day. How can I forgive you?'

Her hands felt hot. Looking at her dishevelled hair and pale face, I hated myself. I slapped myself hard on the cheek.

Zhao Yue grasped my hands. 'Don't do that, Chen Zhong. Don't! I feel sad too.'

We talked calmly about dividing our property. I wanted her to have the apartment. She said that I should take it. I said I could move back in with my parents but that she would have nowhere to go. She said, OK, she could give me some money.

I demanded tearfully, 'Zhao Yue, do you really think I want your money? I mean, what money do you have?'

We held each other and cried.

'Let's stay as we are, OK?' I said.

She shook her head. 'If the day ever comes when I can forget about what happened, I'll come back. But now, no matter what you say, I'm determined to divorce. You've hurt me too much.'

We still slept together during this time, but she froze at my touch. When I kissed her she covered her mouth with her hand. She struggled desperately when I tried to take off her pants. Once, after I'd failed to remove them, I got furious.

'Why are you pretending?' I said. 'I've touched every part of your body numerous times. Why won't you — ?'

She interrupted me. 'If someone shat in your bowl, would you still eat from it?'

'No matter whether a turd or good food, you're my wife,' I said. 'This is your duty until we get divorced.'

She stripped off, then lay down on the bed again with her legs and arms spread wide.

'Come and enjoy yourself like you did with that fat woman,' she said.

I collapsed beside her, deflated and ashamed.

Our very first time was at a cheap hotel outside our campus gates. Up until then we'd kissed and touched each other, but Zhao Yue always refused to go all the way. We had a big fight over it.

'You did that with him, why not with me?' I said.

Zhao Yue flamed:'Chen Zhong, you've broken your promise. You said you wouldn't mention it! What am I to you? A bitch or a girlfriend?'

We parted unhappily and she returned to her room without having dinner. She wouldn't see me afterwards, although I called her name from below for ages, driving the old janitor crazy. But the quarrel did seem to have some effect. Three days later she agreed to go to the hotel with me.

Before she undressed she asked seriously, 'Do you mind that I'm not a virgin?'

I was unbuttoning her clothes in a hurry. 'Not at all,' I said.

She smacked my paws and said, 'Stand back and listen! I'm not an easy lay. I'm giving this to you today because I hope you might marry me in the future. Can you do that?'

I was in the violent throes of sexual desire. Hormones were raging through my body. I said without a moment's thought, 'Yes, I can, I can.'

Zhao Yue at once removed her pants. Later she told me that she'd been struggling to control herself as well.

My past came flooding back. I was like a wastrel from a rich family who'd squandered his life until finally he discovered he was penniless.

The clerk at the government office was a kindly middle-aged woman.

'You two look like a perfect match!' she said. 'It's such a pity!'

Zhao Yue blinked furiously, her chest rising and falling.

We'd come prepared with all the materials for our divorce. One at a time I handed over our residence permits, ID cards, marriage certificate and pictures. All the time, my heart felt numb with sadness.

I said to Zhao Yue, 'From now on you're not the head of a household any more.'

She sobbed and pinched my shoulder hard.

Seeing this, the clerk started saying, 'No, no, no, I can't handle this case. It's against the law of heaven.'

I sighed. 'It's no use. We've made up our minds.'

She glared at me fiercely. 'You men don't have any conscience.'

Then she asked Zhao Yue, 'What do you think?'

Zhao Yue, still sobbing, said, 'It's me who wants to get divorced, it has nothing to do with him. Please, just do it.'

This made the clerk cry too.

After signing the divorce agreement, I gave Zhao Yue the pen.

'It's pretty much like "Zhao's Family Rules",' I said.

She trembled and couldn't write a word. She had to lean on the desk. The clerk sensed a final opportunity.

'I'm asking you for the last time. Are you sure?'

Zhao Yue's eyes were full of tears. I said hoarsely, 'You won't have any regrets?'

'This is your first marriage,' the clerk said. 'Think about it!'

Zhao Yue hit my chest with her fist. She didn't care about people watching us.

I said tenderly, 'Let's not divorce, OK? Let's just go home.'

She shook her head silently. Then she wiped away her tears and told the clerk, 'We're determined. Do it now.'

At the critical moment, I squatted on the ground, unable to watch.

Outside it was a bright sunny Chengdu day. As Zhao Yue and I left the registration bureau there were lively crowds on the streets. We walked with them, keeping close to each other, sighing regularly. As we passed the gate of Renmin Park, I saw a fat guy fall over, which made me laugh. My mood suddenly lifted and I asked Zhao Yue if she felt hungry. She followed me into a KFC.

'Are all men unable to help themselves when they see a beautiful woman?' she asked, sucking her straw.

'Yes, mostly. Your entrepreneur lover is just the same.'

Thinking of her lover I felt frustrated and said, 'Since we're divorced now, can't you tell me about that phone call?'

She looked awkward. 'It's definitely not what you thought. There was nothing between us.'

'Will you marry him?'

'What are you talking about?' she said. 'We're just good friends.'

I cheered up. 'Hmm … if you look for a boyfriend again, will you consider me first?' I asked.

She looked down and didn't say anything. Tears fell drop by drop onto her plate. After a long while she said, 'Why are you being so nice to me now it's too late?'

I'd already moved most of my stuff out, apart from a few last books and DVDs. Zhao Yue silently packed these items for me, putting them into a big bag. I picked it up and started to walk out. But when she called my name, I turned around. She ran her hand through my hair, saying tenderly, 'Take good care of yourself.'

I couldn't bear it any more and took her firmly in my arms.

When my mother found out what had happened, she didn't have the heart to cook for several days. She spent the whole time sighing, which depressed me no end. I locked myself in my room and listened to music and read. Whenever I thought about Zhao Yue, I had this stabbing pain. Downstairs, the old folks were competing to see who could go the longest without speaking and sigh the loudest. Recently I'd noticed that my father was going really grey. I guessed that I wasn't a good son at all. Although I was almost thirty years old, I still made them worry about me.

After dinner, Zhao Yue called and asked if I was OK.

I said yes, then asked, 'Can I sleep at home tonight?'

Her answer was a firm no, and I allowed myself an ironic smile. Once she used to beg me to come home. After that I felt depressed again.

The old man knocked on the door and walked in with a big forced smile on his face. 'Baby Rabbit, wanna play Go?' he said.

My father was still an appalling player. After only a few rounds I'd wiped out most of his pieces. This time he admitted his defeat. He wanted to comfort me but didn't know how. While we sat in awkward silence, Bighead Wang called.

'I never thought she'd really divorce you,' he said. 'I knew she was no good!'

Anger surged in me. 'Shut your stinking mouth. It has nothing to do with her.'

He laughed. 'Hee hee, I know you're feeling down. We're on the second floor at Zero Point! Come over. Getting drunk is the best cure for the blues.'

'Is Li Liang there?' I said.

'Yes. He suggested I call you.'

CHAPTER TWENTY

My mother had heard about this dating agency that would introduce me to potential girlfriends. Initially I said I'd have nothing to do with it.

'What century is this? Can't I find choose for myself?' I said.

My mother harumphed. 'The kind of trash you choose cheats you out of your property and plays with your feelings.'

Recently she'd developed a grudge against Zhao Yue. The week before she'd gone with my sister to visit her, hoping to bring about a reconciliation. What she hadn't expected was to find Zhao Yue having an apparently intimate discussion with a man. My sister said that my mother shook and let fly a few sarcastic words.

She was still cursing when she got home, saying that

Zhao Yue had an evil heart. 'So many years together as man and wife and she can cast you off as easily as that.'

After that she unscientifically predicted that Zhao Yue's future children would be born deformed.

When I heard about that I was wound up all day. I called Zhao Yue that evening, making an effort to sound upbeat, then asked her whether she had a boyfriend. Zhao Yue said she was currently conducting interviews, but this time she'd be sure to look for someone with moral qualities. I laid into her for disloyalty.

'Didn't you say you would consider me first?'

She sighed. 'Sometimes you're very naive. Do you really think we have any chance of getting back together?'

After that I slumped on the sofa and didn't speak for a long time.

My mother kept on at me to divide my property from Zhao Yue's. She helped me do the reckoning. Deposit on the house: 120,000, of which I'd put up 30,000, and the old man had put up 20,000. Furniture: 30,000, all bought by me. Household electrical appliances: 20,000, of which my sister had paid half. The grand total came to more than 70,000, and that wasn't including my monthly mortgage payments.

Immediately after the divorce, I'd told my mother that Zhao Yue was just temporarily taking care of those possessions.

'Whether now or later, it's still mine,' I said.

After this recent incident though, she pressed me to set-tle things.

'If you're embarrassed to talk to her about it, then I will,' she said.

I was suddenly tired of this and fixed my mother with a glare. 'Don't stir, OK? It's hardly very much.'

My throat choked up.

'What money does Zhao Yue have?'

Zhao Yue was broke all through university. At that time my monthly living expenses were around 400 yuan, while she just had 150. With the university's monthly subsidy of 49 yuan 5 mao, she just about scraped by. Later, she told me sadly that when she saw her class-mates buying expensive clothes she would hide inside her mosquito net. When I heard this I felt very sorry for her. At the end of our final year of university, I spent 300 yuan on a grey suit for her. Zhao Yue was so moved that she gripped my hand really hard. That was the spring of 1994. The ori-ental cherry tree was in full bloom, and Zhao Yue and I embraced in the grove behind the campus auditorium, full of confidence about life. But seven years later, that grey suit was rags,; just like the passionate feelings we'd once shared.

My mother set me up with a total of four dates. Each had very distinct peculiarities. The first had a figure like a weight-lifter. I drank tea with her for a while, then fled, making the excuse that something had come up at work. My mother asked how it went.

'There's no way I could ever fight with her,' I explained. 'Just imagine your son with a bloody face every day.'

The second was better-looking, but caked in make-up. Her hair was like a helmet. Straightaway she asked whether I had a house, or a car. I replied that I had a bike and I'd had to borrow money to buy it. Her face froze over.

Each time I went for one of these 'interviews', my mother urged me to describe myself as 'briefly married'. The implication was that my marriage hadn't made any lasting impression on me. I wondered gloomily what the final significance of those three years would turn out to be: a joke, a game, or a wound that would never heal? After going through all that, would I ever dare to go back for a second try?

Li Liang said that marriage and prostitution were the same thing, the only difference being that one was whole-sale and the other was retail. That made me feel even more gloomy and depressed.

That night at Zero Point the three of us got through twenty-three bottles of San Miguel beer. Some time after midnight Li Liang called this young girl who was studying tourism. She was heart-stoppingly beautiful. Li Liang embraced her openly.

'She's very free,' he said. 'Life is for happiness, you don't have to get hung-up on principles.' He kissed her face. 'Am I right?'

The girl nodded shyly.

Glass in hand, I looked at the dance floor's sparkling lights. A long-haired handsome dude was crooning softly:

Come a bit nearer
The bunch of flowers has withered.
Come a bit closer,
You can see my eyes are full of tears.

I considered my friend Li Liang. His eyes shone as brightly as ten years ago, but his face had a coldness to it. Leaning back drunkenly in my chair, I asked myself: where is the future we hoped for?

If you look too closely at things
They'll burn your eyes to dust.
—Li Liang, 'Paradise'.

Li Liang and Ye Mei were finished. As he told me about it, he fixed me with a contemptuous stare.

Bighead Wang said hurriedly, 'Drink, drink. Tonight no one is allowed to talk about anything bad. I won't allow it.'

I'd always dismissed Bighead as mediocre. The strange thing was though, in all these years nothing bad had ever really happened to him. He'd never taken a wrong turn in life. Aside from pure luck, he must possess some life wisdom.

Li Liang said he was Monkey King dressed up as Pig. Bighead Wang looked embarrassed.

'I'm not like you,' he said, 'I don't set my sights too high. As long as I have something to drink during the day and something to grope at night then I'm happy.'

I'd heard that he was pushing hard for another promotion. He wanted to become procurement manager—a famously lucrative post.

Li Liang said enviously, 'It's easier for you to make money than me. There's no risk and you don't even have to use your brain.'

Bighead Wang pretended to be offended. 'I'm a public servant. It doesn't matter what I eat or drink, but I daren't go on the take.'

I interrupted him bad-temperedly. 'Well, that 300,000 you used to buy a house didn't fall from heaven.'

Li Liang backed me up. 'That's right, exactly. Are you saying the five-grain alcohol in your house was just pissed out by you?'

After delivering his punishment that night at the Kaisa Hotel, Li Liang had smiled at me. In the dim lamplight I couldn't be sure what kind of smile it was. I'd called him numerous times since then, wanting to ask for his forgiveness, his pardon. I thought there were very few important things in this world, one of which was Li Liang's friendship. But each time he hung up without listening to me.

On my desk was a photo of our dormitory gang: the Great Wall of 1993. Li Liang had his arm around my shoulder, and I was pinching Bighead Wang's cheek. Chen Chao stood like a blockhead to the side. Big Brother, who then had a bull-like physique but was now dead, was savouring a cigarette. Eight years on I could still hear Li Liang's voice saying, 'From now on we should share our joys and sorrows, face our difficulties together.'

Big Brother chipped in: 'Screw girls together.'

Everyone laughed.

Eight years on, I stared at the photo with something like awe. I'd never believed in fate, but at that moment I found myself wondering who had changed the youthful lives in that photo. Who was it who had divided us onto the two banks of life and death? Or, seeing as my crotch still slightly ached, who'd let Li Liang kick me in the balls?

I often asked myself, if Li Liang didn't have so much money would I respect him so much? Really, I didn't have a clue.

That evening we overdid the drinking. Hardly able to stand, I staggered to the restroom. There I clung to the basin like a beached fish struggling for its last gasp of water. The attendant put a hot towel on my neck and gave me a massage. Suddenly I remembered the days when I'd lie on the sofa and let Zhao Yue pull my ears.

Back at the table I downed another bottle, then stood up and said that I wanted to go and see Zhao Yue. Bighead Wang pushed me down into the chair. He said: 'Fuck you, have a little sense, OK.'

My lips wobbled and the alcohol rushed to my head

again. I felt humiliated. Li Liang was also drunk. He sat there with a stupid smile on his face, but then seeing the look on mine he laughed so much that he fell to the floor. His hot companion made an effort to help him up, but he pushed her away.

'Go, go with my older brother,' he said. 'I'm putting him in your care.'

The girl looked hurt and Li Liang grinned. Then he came out with something even more poisonous.

'Don't play the innocent. Aren't you already thinking of the money? If I gave you 10,000, are you saying you wouldn't do it?'

The music that night at Zero Point was loud, the lights blinding. On the second floor, one person was crying—Chen Zhong. Another laughed—his rival in love, his friend. Outside, Chengdu was like a crematorium. Once in a while there were flickers of starlight, the phosphorescence of those smiling and crying people slowly moving towards the vault of death, like ants on their way to the grave.

CHAPTER TWENTY-ONE

The big boss of our company fancied himself as a poet. Every year on 8 July they held a Company Day Festival, and a few idiots stood on the podium reading his doggerel with great emotion. All that 'Ah Great River, ah Yellow River' shit—enough to make people curl up and die of embarrassment. When I saw the *Festival Poems* that Head Office circulated each year, I couldn't help laughing. Boss Sun took me to task for this: 'Chen Zhong you should watch your attitude. After all, when all is said and done he pays your bills. How about showing some respect?'

I'd adopted an expression of deep solemnity, as if I was parting with the remains of the dead.

This particular boss was widely regarded as brilliant. Company managers at all levels gushed admiration for him. One edition of the *Festival Poems* included a photo of the guy. He seemed about the same age as me, with piercing eyes. Some calligraphy hung in his office: *Raising a person is like raising an eagle.* This meant that a boss must keep staff at the right level of hunger. If an eagle was too well fed, then it would fly away. If starved, then it might bite its owner. I didn't know how other colleagues felt about our company's HR policy, but after seeing this I was certainly disillusioned.

On Monday afternoon I received a call from the big boss's secretary at Head Office. She said the big boss was coming to Chengdu on Wednesday and had scheduled one hour to talk to me. I was to go to the Holiday Inn to pay my respects. When I heard this, I started jumping up and down with excitement. It seemed I hadn't written that report on my work for nothing.

As soon as I'd hung up, Boss Liu from the HR department called my mobile. He advised me to watch details such as wearing a tie, and not eating onion, garlic or smelly tofu beforehand. I thanked him for his kindness and couldn't help feel that my bad luck was over. It was as if the immortals were protecting me. Boss Liu revealed that after the big boss had finished reading my work report, he'd written the following comment: *A person of ability is hard to come by, we should sharpen his wings.* Apparently this legendary boss wasn't so dumb after all.

During our conversation, Fatty Dong was eavesdropping outside my door. When I looked through the transparent screen and saw his fat arse wriggling around, I gritted my teeth. 'Die, Fatty. The time for your reckoning will soon be here.'

Boss Liu from HR was another company legend, a survivor who'd been promoted and demoted several times. Once he'd been demoted from director of sales to a clerk with a monthly basic salary of just 90 yuan, but he came through it. Trial by adversity was our company culture: knock someone down, then see what they were made of. If they could come back they were talented, but if they sank quickly they were a waste of space.

Fatty Dong was still being watched closely by his ugly wife. She would check up on him a couple of times a day, then after work he had to report home at a given hour. He was forbidden to take part in any business entertainment. A few days before, Old Lai, a client from Chongqing had come to Chengdu on a business trip. Old Lai was one of our major clients whose business was worth more than 10 million a year. Although he said it was a business trip, it was actually just an excuse for a pleasure cruise of eating, drinking, women and music. As he put it, he wanted to 'experience some local culture'. I gave him the use of a company car, arranged for him to stay at the Jinjiang Hotel and escorted him twice to eat at the Gingko and Peony Pavilion. Each time cost more than 3000 yuan, but it could all be claimed back on expenses. On the final night, Old Lai returned the hospitality and said that I should invite Boss Dong as well. When I gave Fatty a call, he wheezed and said that his wife wouldn't let him, This amused the client and he said Fatty Dong was a potato head. I wasn't quite sure what he meant by that.

Fatty Dong was very likely still getting beaten up. The previous few days had been unbearably hot, but he continued to wear long-sleeved shirts and he moved very gingerly. I quipped to Zhou Weidong: 'Behind every fat face is a bloody arse.' He laughed so much his false tooth almost fell out.

On 1 June, Children's Day, the company organised a party, arranging for all the workers in the company to go to One Hundred Flowers Park to play mahjong. Zhou Weidong and I sat at the same table. We'd just started playing when I got a full flush. At that moment, I heard Fatty Dong's voice at the next table: 'Fuck him, reporting me to the police and telling my wife. That's too poisonous.'

I lifted my head and saw both him and Liu Three staring at me murderously.

Once things had quietened down after the prostitute incident, Fatty Dong started to look for opportunities to take a shot at me. The previous Friday, just before clock-off time, the accountant furtively slipped me a report. She said that Fatty Dong had made her write it, and they'd already faxed it to Head Office's finance department. I looked at the report and started sweating. Bloody Fatty Dong had deliberately found the most sensitive spot to stick in the knife: the subject of the report was 'Concerning Chen Zhong's Excessive Debt Problem Settlement Method'. One of its headings was: *Legal Recourse*. I roundly cursed all his family members, young and old. Suddenly there were stormclouds overhead again and my insides were burning.

The big boss looked rather coquettish in a checked open-necked shirt. He wore slippers as he paced the room, his hands held behind his back. There was a faint scent of perfume on him and I suspected this guy might have recently broken some of the People's Republic of China's fundamental laws.

The boss asked me some questions about the current market situation, the company's management problems and Fatty Dong's leadership qualities. Having prepared thoroughly, I talked non-stop for over an hour. The boss listened and occasionally interjected a few comments. The interview seemed to be finished, then he asked me: 'Are you willing to work at Head Office?'

I realised that if I went to Head Office, that might really be the end for Zhao Yue and me.

On 15 July it was the one-month anniversary of our divorce. I hurried straight back to the apartment after work and opened the door with the key that I'd secretly kept. I crept in furtively. Zhao Yue wasn't back from work yet, but the room was full of familiar things. The gleaming tiles illuminated my sallow face. Her underwear was drying on the balcony. When I held it up to my nose and sniffed, it had a faint but familiar fragrance. There was a half-eaten fish in the fridge. I used my fingers to pick off a piece but found it slightly bland. Whenever I ate Zhao Yue's food, I always had to add some sauce or vinegar, and I'd often lectured

her with the cautionary tale of the white feather girl. 'If you don't eat enough salt your pubes will turn white,' I'd tell her, and then she'd hit me.

I sat on the sofa and leafed through a photo album. All the pictures with me in them had been removed; there were just a few left of Zhao Yue by herself. My hands trembled as I hugged the pillow I'd once slept on and let two soundless teardrops fall.

By half seven, Zhao Yue still hadn't returned. I called and reminded her that today was the anniversary of our divorce.

'I'll treat you to dinner,' I said.

She said she was eating right now. 'Join me,' she said. 'I'll introduce you to a friend.'

'Is it your boyfriend?' I asked.

She laughed, but wouldn't say either way.

My temper flared, and I said, 'Where are you? I'll come at once.'

They were at the newly opened Chongqing Hotpot Restaurant at Nijia Bridge. There was a hubbub of voices inside, and the heat and fumes were overwhelming. Two guys at the next table had their sleeves rolled up exposing fatty flesh like a pig's arse.

Zhao Yue did the introductions: 'Yang Tao, Chen Zhong.'

He had a slightly superior expression. I gave the guy a sly look. On such a hot day he was still wearing a tie. Frowning, I said to Zhao Yue, 'Why did you choose a lousy place like this? It's hot enough to die.'

The guy's neck stiffened.

Zhao Yue poured me some wine. 'Mind your own

business,' she said. 'This was my choice.'

Feeling depressed, I took a swig from my glass. After a while, I said to Yang Tao, 'Do you have a business card?'

I was thinking that if he turned out to be the guy on the telephone, I would have to kill him.

He came on all prickly, saying that he never used business cards. 'If you want to remember someone's name, you don't need a card. If you don't want to remember, then it doesn't make any difference.'

I said to Zhao Yue, 'Don't you think the food here is a bit peppery?' And then I spat on the floor.

Yang Tao's face quickly froze.

He pulled out a Red Pagoda cigarette and I produced a Marlboro. He wore a domestic Peng brand shirt, I wore Hugo Boss. His phone was the Motorola 7689, mine was the V8088+. At his side was a darkish canvas bag. Mine was a genuine Dunhill, which even discounted had cost more than 3000 yuan. From where I sat, the top of his head was just on my line of sight, so I estimated he must be at least three inches shorter than me. After I'd finished this analysis, my anger became even more intense.

I looked at Zhao Yue with a caring expression and asked her how she'd been recently.

She said, 'The same as always, how else?'

I bragged that I was about to be promoted to general manager. 'You won't need to ride a bicycle,' I told her. 'I'll pick you up every day in my Honda Accord.'

Zhao Yue was very happy. 'I just knew you'd be a success,' she said.

'Come on, cheers. Cheers.'

She leaned over and we clinked glasses. Meanwhile Yang Tao was fixated on the goose intestines in the hotpot. The chopsticks in his hand trembled violently.

Zhao Yue said that Yang Tao was the CEO of some stinking company or other. A 'small boss'.

I said, 'I've seen a few bosses, but never such a "small boss" before.' She gave me a hard look. 'That's a funny way to talk.'

I quickly apologised.

'Wife, wife, forgive me. From now on I will wash the dishes every day.'

I'd said these words to her once after an argument. Zhao Yue laughed but then made a serious face and told me: 'Watch what you're saying. Who's your wife?'

I smiled, then gave Yang Tao a smirk, thinking, you just don't have what it takes to compete with me.

When we'd just about finished eating, I called the waitress for the bill. Yang Tao at once produced a wad of hundreds from his canvas bag.

'I'm getting this,' he said. 'No discussion, OK.'

I mocked him. 'You don't need to pull out so much money and shock people. It's cheap here, right? We can each pay our share.'

Zhao Yue tried to calm things down, but the guy was finally losing it.

'Say what you like, I'm a CEO. I'm a bit better off than you two.'

'I've never seen so much money myself,' I replied, 'but

each month the value of the goods passing through my hands is around twenty million.'

Despite this satirical blow, I still felt I hadn't wound him up enough, and so I said: 'Only assholes try to impress people with money.'

I grabbed his hand to immobilise it, then took 200 yuan from my wallet and gave it to the waitress. Perhaps I used more force than I'd realised. Yang Tao struggled. 'You bastard,' he said.

I took exception to that and kicked him to the ground, then tried to strangle him with his tie. I punched him on the bridge of his nose and said: 'Do you still want to fuck with me?'

People crowded round. Yang Tao lay on the ground. His bloody nose was the colour of red pepper oil, but his mouth still cursed me. I hadn't worked off all my anger so I aimed another punch at the left side of his face.

'Screw you!'

Whenever Zhao Yue witnessed violence, she'd freeze to the spot. She reacted that way when that group of hooligans attacked her, and it was the same now as I beat up Yang Tao. She sat there, mouth open but unable to speak. I threw Yang Tao aside with a sickening thud and went to get my bag. I said triumphantly to Zhao Yue, 'Come on. Let's go home.'

At this Zhao Yue finally revived. She unclenched her hands and bent down to Yang Tao, giving him some napkins to wipe his face. As she helped him, she was crying. I was mad with jealousy, furious that I couldn't rip Yang Tao to pieces.

'He insulted me first!' I protested.

Zhao Yue suddenly slapped me hard on the face. I just gaped at her. She stood in the middle of the crowd, her long hair waving, her lovely eyes full of tears.

'Get lost,' she said. 'Just beat it.'

CHAPTER TWENTY-TWO

Lengjia Temple Middle School hadn't changed much over the years. The potholed road was lined by short, dilapidated buildings. Exhausted, I slowly made my way up to the primary school. The night was pitch black, and my mates had gone home. A dim light glimmered at the top of the main building. I was filled with pleasurable melancholy, as if I'd just lost something important but sensed it was still close by. Someone was approaching pushing a bicycle and strangely I noticed a big lump of pork tied to it. I leapt aside into a clump of trees to let him pass.

A sudden powerful force made me lose my balance. Something grabbed my foot and pulled me to the ground. I tried to cry out, but couldn't. Although I wanted to resist, I couldn't move even my little finger. My body was powerless, only my eyes could move.

'Let me go!' I implored. 'I haven't done anything wrong.'

The force dissolved with a blare of sound, then right in front of me I saw a pile of fresh black shit. A dog, half the height of a man, was eyeing my throat hungrily…

My father was battering the bedroom door.

'Rabbit, Rabbit, what's up?'

Suddenly I was awake, sweating. My heart was thumping. After I'd composed myself a little, I managed to say, 'Everything's fine. I just had a dream. You go to sleep.'

The old man didn't leave but paced outside my door, his sandals clattering. Then he said, 'You were crying very loudly. Is there really nothing wrong?'

Moved by his concern, I opened the door and let him in. We lit cigarettes and then sat there in silence. Outside, dawn was breaking; from far away came the sound of the water-sprinkler car's bell.

When my father had finished his cigarette, he patted my shoulder and said, 'Sleep. Don't let your imagination run away with you. Tomorrow you still have to go to work.'

That first month or so after my divorce, I did overtime almost every day. Not only was I trying to win a promotion, I was deliberately losing myself in work. My contacts with several big companies proved fruitful and we signed a number of contracts. I estimated that this month the repair centre's service revenues would be up by about twenty per cent. The petrol situation had also taken a turn for the better. Our adverts from the previous month had paid off, and sales had almost returned to the same level as the same period the previous year.

My brother-in-law had a friend who worked on the Chengyu expressway and through him I got thirty free advertisement spots. I gave him 2000 yuan in a red envelope, then got 23,000 from the company—a profit of over 20,000. Suddenly my wallet was full again. With all my achievements, Fatty Dong didn't dare to fart in my direction, much as he would have loved to. The best he could do was write that report on my debt problem.

One day though, Zhou Weidong told me that the office's Little Wang had created a case file on me. This concerned me a little. I called Boss Liu and honestly admitted my error, saying that I was willing to accept the company's disciplinary action.

'It's good that you have this attitude,' he said, and told me to work hard and not worry. He promised to talk to the accounts department. A few days later, a ruling on my debt problem came down, suggesting that the Sichuan branch 'use its discretion'. The ruling proposed two methods of resolution: one was to repay the debt in instalments; the second was to deduct fifty per cent of my salary each month until everything had been repaid. At once I felt the weight of anxiety lift. I couldn't stop smiling, and I thought Die, Fatty! Let's see what tricks you have up your sleeve now.

At the end of July he wanted to promote Liu Three to be deputy sales manager, but I adamantly refused. Secretly I pressed several of our clients to report that Liu Three had no ability. The odds were stacked against him from the start because I'd cultivated those guys for a long time with drinks and money. They'd do what I asked. This tactic was very effective and people paid even less attention to stinking Liu Three. Without my approval, no one would listen to him.

I had this sensation that I was going over to the dark side. When I thought back to the fight in the restaurant I was beside myself. Because of bloody Yang Tao, Zhao Yue hated me, and had even slapped me in front of a crowd. All those years I'd never once lifted a finger to her, but now she slapped me. That slap on the face had cooled my heart right down. It made me realise that all relationships were the same. What the hell was love between man and wife? What was growing old together? The truth was a load of dog shit. Divorce, the end of life? What a joke.

It was Zhao Yue's birthday, 26 July. Each year I bought her a big bunch of roses. This year, however, I could economise. I guessed Zhao Yue wasn't short of people to buy her flowers, in particular that cheap low-life Yang Tao. When Zhao Yue got his flowers, she'd have a cheap smile as well, superficial as hell. This image depressed me, and so I gave Bighead Wang a call.

'Does the station chief have time for a drink?' I asked.

He blew his police whistle and came straightaway. He had a lot of power now. All the procurement for the precinct was managed by him. There was a rumour he was considering ordering twenty VW Passats and was asking everywhere about prices.

'I might be able to help,' I told him. 'It just depends if you have the guts.'

This guy loved money more than life. Last time, when I got those government car plates for him, he'd sold them on and made more than 2000. When he saw me afterwards he didn't even give me the table scraps. Now he said that my proposal would be difficult for him.

'I've only just been promoted so I should play it straight for a few years.'

'You bastard!' I said. 'Don't play the bureaucrat with me. After doing this you'll have at least 10,000 profit. Do we have a deal?'

'What price?'

I told him he wouldn't have a problem with it. I had the car business pretty well sussed. My sister ran a stall in the Qingyang automobile showroom. Every day she went to work on people's brains: *Want a car or not? Lowest prices in all Chengdu.*

'She knows the trade inside out,' I told Bighead. 'How to make money from cars, how to make money from car plates, how to make money from insurance. In the past, when business was good, she'd easily make more than 10,000 profit a month. In the last two years, however, things haven't been so hot. My sister often sighs that selling cars isn't as good as selling tofu.'

Bighead was interested. 'Well, what are we waiting for?' he said. 'Let's agree to that. Of course, we won't let your sister help us for nothing.'

I drained my glass, thinking, You bastard. I just knew you couldn't resist the sugar-coated bullet. Of course we won't let her help for nothing. Do you think I'm Lei Feng?[17]

I'd often thought that Fatty Dong and Bighead Wang could have been brothers. Their physical appearance, way of talking and body language were very similar. What was more, they were both equally mean. Li Liang said that Bighead had cupboards full of five-grain alcohol at home. He never opened them when we were round. Apparently Bighead's father had opened a liquor store by the banks of the Funan River, selling top-quality booze and cigarettes. It seemed likely that most of his supply came from Station Chief Wang's stockpile of corrupt gains. When Bighead was dating Lan Lan, Li Liang summed things up in a way that always made me smile: 'Xian's wallet is tight, Chong-qing's trousers are slack.'

Zhang Lan Lan was from Chongqing. According to Big-head Wang, they slept together on their second date.

Li Liang and I agreed however that Bighead had changed for the better in the last few years. If you needed it, he would help with anything. Anything, that was, except money. In the time I'd been a manager, I'd helped him get car plates and petrol coupons and got his car fixed, basi-cally all for free. He'd made at least 20 or 30,000 out of this, but he wasn't at all grateful. Last time we played mahjong at his house, I was cleaned out and asked to borrow a few hundred yuan. He was very grudging.

The bar was buzzing. A group of gorgeous girls squeezed past us. Their fragrant flesh assailed my nostrils; their eyes were vacant. They were certainly prostitutes, but one of them looked a lot like Zhao Yue from behind. I frowningly reflected that right now she was probably having another candlelit dinner, smiling at god knows who. Whoever he was, I wished I could kick him. I lit a cigarette, thinking, Fuck you. From now on, I don't have any ties to anyone. Except for Ma and Pa, my only family is money.

My parents' hearts had been broken by the calamity I'd suffered. They tried to hide it, and put on angelic smiles whenever they saw me, which was upsetting. It made me thoroughly depressed. Secretly I'd rented a place in the Xiyan district, planning to move there at the weekend and escape them.

Meanwhile, I'd discovered that my first ever conquest—that girl Pang Yuyan—was now an uncouth hussy. The previous Tuesday I'd gone to Scholar's Cap Street to pick up a spare part for the repair factory. In the distance, I saw a crowd gathering. A woman was verbally attacking some guy, describing in great detail his mother's genitalia. This made me uncomfortable. When I'd concluded my business and came out again, the fat woman was still cursing the guy, casting doubt on his parentage, with lots of details about how his mother had copulated with all

kinds of birds and beasts. I thought it was a real waste
that this woman had never become a film director. Moving closer, I gave her an appreciative smile. We were both
struck dumb. Ten years suddenly rolled back and I had
a vision of her leaning against an electricity pylon eating
watermelon seeds with a big bad smile. I saw her lying
stark naked on Lang Four's bed, giving me my first ever
physiognomy class step by step. I saw her running away
from a beating by her old man; hiding behind the rubbish
bins in the backyard.

'Is it you?' I shouted.

Pang Yuyan blushed and at once fled through the wall
of people. In just a twinkling of an eye she'd disappeared,
just like twenty years ago when dressed in all her finery
she'd burst out of the room where I'd had my sexual ini-
tiation and giggled to Lang Four, 'Baby Rabbit is really a
tender chicken.' After that she ran off embarrassed, leaving
me not knowing whether to laugh or cry.

That afternoon, bathed in the bright sunlight of
Chengdu, I asked myself over and over exactly who it was
who had been witness to my youth. Was it the slim viva-
cious girl or this foul-mouthed harridan?

Bighead Wang supposed that I was thinking of Zhao Yue.
His face disdainful, he said, 'How come you're acting like a
young girl? Divorced is divorced. Start looking for someone
else!'

'Fuck you, just drink and shut up,' I replied.

Bighead Wang drained his glass in one gulp, then seemed to remember something he wanted to ask me.

'Did you know that Li Liang … ,' he started. But then the girls came squeezing past us again and Bighead Wang immediately shut up and stared at them instead. One girl pressed her chest against me as she nudged past, and it was soft with a warm fragrance.

After they'd gone, I said bad-temperedly, 'Li Liang what? Hurry up and tell me.'

He drank some beer, then said softly, 'Did you know that Li Liang is on drugs?'

CHAPTER TWENTY-THREE

In our final term at university, our campus was filled with a fin de siècle craziness. Sweethearts faced with approaching separation smiled like spring flowers or cried like rain. No one was willing to let these final moments slip away as they worked out their final passions on their lovers' bodies. The woods around our campus were strewn with condoms. Everyone's directions had been set; the future wound away into the distance. Happy expressions concealed our anxiety. Bighead Wang spent all his days sunk in drink, while Big Brother rode his bicycle into town each afternoon to watch porn films.

We all neglected Li Liang though. After his third unsuccessful relationship he'd become unusually dejected and had even given up studying. Every day he played mahjong, his hair dishevelled, his face unwashed, squandering his allowance and running up debts. Several times I tried to give him advice, but he was very negative and wouldn't listen.

'Fuck it, why can't you tell me something interesting?' he'd say.

One night, after lights out, Big Brother was providing his customary blow-by-blow account of the porn movies he'd seen that day. Our minds exploded as he vividly described luscious girls in every kind of position, doing oral, anal, etc. After a while, Chen Chao couldn't control himself any longer. With a loud cry he leapt up, grabbed a bucket and hurried to the wash room to douse himself in cold water. Two minutes later he was back.

'Chen Zhong, come quick. Li Liang ... ,' he called from the doorway.

We were just one month from graduation. Qi Yan was already dead; we'd helplessly watched her life drain away. Number Six dorm's Zhang Jun had long since become dust, the moonlight coldly illuminating his empty bed. As I raced along the long, gloomy corridor, I had a bad feeling about this. I found Li Liang slumped against the cistern, not moving. His head lolled on his chest. His toothbrush and soap had fallen to the ground and the tap was still running.

'Li Liang, what's up?' I said.

He didn't move. Chen Chao checked his breathing, then said with an ashen face, 'Mother! Li Liang is dead.'

I gave him a ferocious look, then hauled Li Liang up by his hands and feet and started dragging him. I was shitting myself because the body in my arms had no warmth, none.

His limbs were rigid, there was no heartbeat and no sign of breathing.

With great difficulty we got him back to the dorm, where I tried to revive him. Big Brother helped me heave Li Liang onto the bed and we looked at each other in panic.

That was the first time. Later, at a small restaurant outside the school, Li Liang passed out again. From that day on I had an intuition that Li Liang would die alone.

I hadn't been to his house for ages. People were hypocrites, I thought. While the illusion was convenient they could be friends, but once reality surfaced they would fight tooth and claw. 'Undying love' between a man and woman sounded great; so did 'eternal friendship'; but who knew what the person in your arms was really thinking when they were making those pledges of friendship or love?

Bighead said that he'd seen Li Liang shoot up.

'His arm is full of track marks. It's terrifying.'

He furrowed his brow in disgust. I was devastated, and furious with Bighead Wang for not telling me sooner. He said Li Liang wouldn't let him.

'You shouldn't get involved,' he added. 'Li Liang himself said it's the only pleasure he has left.'

Bighead was unusually emotional. He grabbed his beer glass and hurled it to the floor. People at the surrounding tables stared at us alarmed.

'Fuck you, what are you looking at?' Bighead yelled.

When Li Liang wasn't in the grip of his addiction though,

he was the same as usual. He listened to music, read books and studied the futures market on the internet.

'Give it up,' I told him. 'Sleeping with whores or gambling aren't such a big deal, but once you get involved with drugs, you're finished.'

He hit a key to change the screensaver on his computer, then said, 'You know why Ye Mei slept with you?'

I lowered my head. 'I was wrong. Don't bring it up again.'

He swung round to face me.

'It's not all your fault,' he said. 'You see, I can't get it up.'

For ages I couldn't say anything.

He turned back to his computer, saying calmly, 'I've had this problem for more than ten years; it's ok. Yesterday I called Chen Chao and told him straight out: my little brother is on strike.'

I felt terrible for him. Awkwardly I asked whether he'd been to the hospital.

'It's no good,' he said. 'When I was small, my father kicked me and that caused the problem.'

He stood up and paced behind my back, laughing crudely. 'You know, Chen Zhong, that day I desperately wanted to do the same to you.'

That first day at university, Li Liang was the last of our dormitory crew to show up. The Sichuan hall monitor was concerned; he told us that our floor should have another Sichuan student and we should take special care of him. That night at twelve, Li Liang knocked lightly on the door and said in a strong Sichuan accent: 'Fellow students, please open the door. I'm down for this dormitory too.'

Suppressing our mirth, we opened the door to let him in. The Li Liang of 1991 wore a pair of grey trousers and carried an enormous travel bag. His face had a slightly shy expression. 1991's Bighead Wang was asleep and snoring like thunder, a fat hand across his stomach. 1991's Chen Zhong was wearing just undershorts as he shook Li Liang's hand. On 15 September 1991, as far as I remember, there was no war. Nobody famous died. A few babies were born and, on their first sight of the world, began to cry loudly. No one knew how their lives would turn out, but it was said they were all spirits from heaven.

Trying to persuade Li Liang to quit smack was impossible. He was well aware of all the logical arguments, and always cut directly to the ultimate question: 'If you only had one month to live, would you do drugs or not?'

I thought about it seriously, then answered, yes, I would.

He smiled. 'In my view, there's not much difference between one month and ten years. Life shouldn't be a test that you copy out over and over again. Do you understand?'

'I'm confused,' I said. 'All I know is that smack is bad for you. Haven't you seen those addicts? They all look like ghouls.'

He dragged me before a mirror. He said, 'Look at yourself.'

Yes, I was emaciated. My face was pallid, my hair dishevelled. My eyes were red and puffy, and there were hairs growing from my nose. I didn't know when the corners of my eyes had got those lines. On one side of my nose were two black spots like fly shit.

'Look at yourself,' Li Liang said, 'You look like a ghost don't you?'

When I was leaving he said to me, 'Tell Ye Mei. She can have a divorce, but she can't have a cent of my money.'

'You should tell her yourself,' I said. 'I'll never see her again after today.'

He studied me coldly then said, 'Fuck you. She only cares about you now.'

CHAPTER TWENTY-FOUR

Liu Three and Zhou Weidong finally came to blows. I was having an afternoon nap in the office when through my sleep I heard this huge racket. Pushing open the door, I found a crowd of people. Liu Three was pacing tensely, his temples pulsing with veins. Several people were restraining Zhou Weidong, and his hands and feet flailed, and saliva sprayed grotesquely from his mouth. He shouted that he wanted to have carnal relations with Liu Three's mother. Fatty Dong threw his huge weight around and pleaded with Zhou Weidong to calm down. Zhou Weidong wouldn't listen, which made Fatty furious. He turned to me. 'These are all in your team, you should be managing this.'

I replied tartly, 'Isn't Liu Three your lackey? I'm not getting involved, let them go on fighting.'

Zhou Weidong was one metre seventy-eight of

intimidating might, so even two Liu Threes together couldn't beat him up.

Fatty Dong looked grave. 'Good, I've noted your attitude,' he said, and clenching his jaw, marched into his office. I guessed he was going to write up a report.

I wasn't scared of Fatty Dong, because just then my hands were around his throat. On the day Head Office had made suggestions for handling my debt problem, we were having one of our regular meetings. The accountant passed the comments to Fatty Dong and the jerk was so enraged it seemed he might have an apoplexy. Forgetting the basic principle of not bringing disaster on yourself by shooting your mouth off, he muttered that Head Office were all idiots, and then quipped sardonically to Liu Three: 'Seems Head Office encourages the embezzlement of company money. You should borrow a few thousand too, and blow it on whores and gambling.'

'Write down Boss Dong's suggestions,' I told Zhou Weidong.

The guy quickly made a show of noting it down. Fatty Dong realised that he'd forgotten himself and his face turned white.

Liu Three had been having a hard time lately. The week before I'd asked him to go to Chongqing to settle some bad accounts. It was a bitch of an assignment and Liu Three pleaded that he didn't want to go. I said, 'If you don't want to go then just hand in your resignation.' He got in his car angrily. The value of the Chongqing disputed accounts was in the region of 400,000 or more, and they went back to the dawn of time, 1999. Since then the company had restructured its finance department several times so the accounts were in a real mess. No one could tell which were real and which were false.

Another issue was that the client had an unbelievably bad temper. If you said anything he didn't like, his face immediately clouded over and then he'd explode. Liu Three also had a foul temper. He frequently banged the desk in clients' offices and got his ear bitten off, and then would go crying to Fatty Dong for help, saying that I'd framed him.

As soon as Liu Three had got in his car, I called the client and asked him to set up something to make Liu Three look bad.

'No problem,' he said. 'I always thought that kid was an ugly bastard.'

When the client had come to Chengdu to experience 'local culture' he'd been extremely satisfied with the hospitality he'd received. Later he asked me to help him hook up with a girl he'd met before at the Jinjiang Hotel, called Bai Xiaowen or something. I could tell from his voice that he really wanted her in his arms again.

In 'places of entertainment' the girls very rarely used their own names. I got a friend to do some investigating, and found there was no such person as Bai Xiaowen. Even her phone number and address were false. When I told him, the guy was surprisingly devastated.

'Big Brother, this was just a one-off transaction,' I told him. 'Don't mistake it for a long-term contract, OK?'

He laughed, and then invited me to Chongqing, saying that the girls there were exceptionally hot. Underneath all the talk, I knew he was looking for a way to keep the disputed thousands. He was always calling to query the account and generally behaving unscrupulously. He was a typical businessman.

When Liu Three returned, I handed him the client's complaint form and asked him what we should do about it.

He looked at me superciliously and said, 'You should go to Chongqing yourself and get the money back. Then if you want to fire me or cut my salary I'll have no objection.'

I'd been to Chongqing numerous times and had plenty of experience of the hot girls, hotpot and hot pepper chicken dishes of Geleshan. Compared with Chengdu, Chongqing was down to earth but coarse, irreverent but edgy. I was there last August and was wandering the streets when I heard a man and a woman talking.

'Why are you walking so fast?' the man said.

The girl replied, 'I need to have a piss.'

I cracked up when I saw the speaker—a fine-figured, beautiful girl.

That night I went to a nightclub and picked a girl who looked like like Gong Li[18]. I groped her a few times and she wasn't happy about it.

'If you want to fuck, then take off your trousers. If you

want to sing, then sit still for a bit,' she snapped at me. 'What are you poking about for?'

I felt ashamed.

This time the client drove to the bus station to meet me. At his side was a girl who resembled a middle school student. I asked whether this was his daughter and he huffed and said it was his new lover. I almost vomited at the thought of that bulging stomach on top of that little girl's body. This guy had violent tendencies. Once when we were at the Orchid Song Hall, a girl complained about his bad breath and he slapped her face and swore at her.

The most obvious change in me since graduation was that I didn't get too worked up about things. At university we'd come up with a summary of the basic requirements to be a 'real man'. Among these were: A real man must come to a woman's defence. Big Brother had his own famous saying: Women are to use, not abuse. To hit a woman is unpardonable.

But because of that possible sales commission, I had to call this bastard a brother, and help him get women. When I thought about it, it really was disgraceful.

We had dinner at the Marriott where the abalone alone cost more than 400 yuan. In between courses Old Lai chatted away constantly, criticising our company. He said our management was weak and our clients suffered. If we continued to provoke him, he wouldn't do business with us anymore.

I said, 'OK, if you want to lose 800,000 profit each year, I'll find someone else.'

He was slightly thrown by my attitude. This was where I was more effective than Liu Three: I didn't just know how to woo clients; I could also beat up on them too when required. Call them 'brother' and needle them at the same time.

He nudged Young Lover, and the teenager poured me a cup of five-grain alcohol. Her fingers were tapered, her skin white and tender. She looked sixteen at the most. Her face was childish and still had an air of shy embarrassment. I couldn't help feeling very sorry for her.

My own intentions of course were far from pure. Of the disputed 400,000 we had a fairly strong claim to about 120,000 which we definitely had to get back. As for the remaining 280,000 I wasn't too bothered whether he gave it back or not, but he at least had to stuff some money in my mouth. This guy was more corrupt than anyone, he should be able to guess what I was up to. The posturing had to be a bluff, to give him some leeway when discussing price. That was all. My ideal sum was 50,000, which would allow him to exchange 280,000 for 50,000. I didn't like to think how many more young girls he could corrupt with those dishonest gains.

After dinner we went to a teahouse. He sent Young Lover away and said to me lewdly, 'How about her? Very tender, yeah?'

'Be careful she's not underage,' I said, 'otherwise you'll go down for years.'

He laughed, and got onto the main subject. 'What are we going to do about that 400,000? You make a suggestion.'

I savoured a mouthful of fragrant maofeng, then smilingly kicked the ball back to him.

'You first. You're the one who's been on me like a dog in heat for over a month. You must have some ideas.'

In the last few years I'd fought hundreds of battles — with suppliers, sales agents, advertising companies, insurance companies. I'd honed my negotiating skills, earning a reputation for toughness, and clients were afraid that I'd come in and give them a lesson too. Often we'd negotiate for a while and then suddenly they'd exclaim: 'How did I get screwed by you yet again!'

Actually, there were only two secrets to success. The first was to let the enemy go first. The second: at all costs disguise the cards in your hand.

My greatest success came when I was discussing replenishing our stock with the spare parts vendor on Scholar's Cap Street. The boss was a thirty-something woman. After we'd signed the contract she almost cried, saying she'd never met anyone as ruthless as me and she'd need to work for a year to recover her losses. This woman was the flower of Scholar's Cap Street. Her husband was twenty years older than her, one of Chengdu's first millionaires. I'd looked at her chest, thinking, If you weren't so loyal to your husband, there's no way I'd leave you feeling empty.

The client claimed our company's accounts were a mess and that we'd issued duplicate bills so that the 400,000 was basically fictitious. He asked us to set things straight and write off the debt. I laughed so much I nearly showered his face with tea.

'Big brother, you must think I'm stupid,' I said. 'If it's really as you say, then why are we sitting here?'

'OK, so what do you suggest we do?' he replied.

I produced a thick pile of documents. 'Here's all the hard evidence: 400,000 yuan and we want it all.'

He looked furious. 'If you just want to fuck me and my family, forget it.'

I knew exactly how to play this game.

'There's nothing I can do,' I told him. 'You see, I'm just an employee. Not a penny of this money goes into my pocket, but I have an obligation to sort this out. You're my big brother; you should show some understanding for your little brother.'

Now we were both clear on each other's intention. I drank tea and waited for his reaction. He muttered for a while, then asked me how much.

'As a minimum you should repay the company 150,000,' I said. 'Of the remaining 250,000, whatever you say is OK.'

'You're clearly presenting me with a false bill,' he said. 'What 250,000? At the most it is 6 or 7000. Let's have half each, OK?'

In what at first appeared to be a digression, I told him a story about the time when Old Sun and I went to Wenjiang sauna. Boss Sun decided to see what it was like to be an emperor and called for one tall and one short girl to come to his room. After negotiations he said he'd pay 1000 all up, which he'd allocate according to the quality of their work. The tall girl was new and not very open. First, she wasn't willing to take off her clothes, and then when Old Sun changed girls halfway through, she asked him to change condom. The old guy didn't have any choice and, despite his curses, put on a new condom. He was about to re-enter the battle scene when he went limp and couldn't get it up again, even with manual stimulation. He fiddled with it for ages, but there was no way the session could go on, which made him absolutely furious. In the end, he gave the short girl the entire 1000. The tall girl thought this unfair and argued with Old Sun. Old Sun said, 'You did nothing to satisfy me, so why should I help you to make money?'

The final sentence was the moral of the story. Old Lai started to laugh, but then, after turning it over in his mind, he looked serious and said, 'You talk too much. If you're not happy about something, tell me outright. What are you getting at?'

I explained: 'Doing business is the same as sex. It's all about satisfying each other's desires so everyone is happy.'

He looked at me half admiringly, half grudgingly, then said, 'OK, last offer: 50,000. If you're still not satisfied then let's settle it through official channels.'

After we'd settled a price, the rest of the issues were easily dealt with — how to make the payment, how to destroy the evidence. I'd worked all this out long ago, and he didn't really have much to add.

I felt pleased with myself: recently I'd managed to dredge up a fair amount of money. Twenty thousand from the billboards, and now 50,000 from this. It was enough for a deposit on a house. When I thought about houses though, I felt a bit sad because I didn't know what

Zhao Yue was doing now in our apartment. I didn't know whether or not there was someone lying in that place where I used to lie, caressing that lovely body I'd caressed so many times.

Young Lover was waiting impatiently outside. She'd come in and disturbed us a few times, then, seeing that we were still talking business, had left without saying anything. Whether intentionally or not, her eyes frequently met mine, making me a little excited.

The client saw this and said with a big smile, 'OK, tonight you take her. I haven't made any other arrangements for you.'

I was surprised by this. Feigning indignation, I reprimanded him. 'What kind of person do you take me for? A real man doesn't take someone's girl. Even if you threatened to cut off my head, I wouldn't do this.'

He lit an extra mellow 555 and said smilingly, 'You don't need to be so false. You've been lusting for her all night— do you think I'm an idiot? Now you're just pretending to be respectable.'

The client gave me a rundown of Young Lover's specialities: 'Her singing voice is voice is very sweet. She's skilled in many techniques and positions, especially cowgirl.'

I looked at Young Lover again, and found her making eyes at me and pouting her lips, like a Japanese cartoon character.

It was raining lightly and there were fewer people on the street than usual. Young Lover opened a small embroidered umbrella. I put my arm around her shoulder as we

slowly walked along. We passed a few uninteresting bou-
tiques. Suddenly she grabbed my hand.

'Brother Chen, will you buy me a skirt? It won't be more
than 100 yuan.'

I felt pity for her. 'Go in and choose,' I said. 'I'll
wait here.'

She ran in eagerly. Within five minutes, she'd tried on
four long skirts. Each time she came out to seek my opinion, asking me whether it looked good or not. I nodded
silently, thinking about the days when I'd browse the shops
on Chunxi Street with Zhao Yue, hand in hand, drawn to
the ones with the most people.

'Does it look good?' Young Lover asked.

I struggled to blink away tears at the thought of another
smiling face. Zhao Yue used to say, 'Does it look good?
What mark would you give it?'

Young Lover ended up with two skirts. Grand total: 260
yuan. Back at the hotel, she put her lips against my ear
and murmured, 'Brother Chen, you're really good to me.
Today, you can do whatever you like.'

My heart was suddenly filled with a hatred that I didn't
really understand. I flung her onto the bed and, saying
nothing, began to rip violently at her clothes. She pushed
me away terrified, and pleaded with me to be careful of the
buttons and zippers.

'You don't need to be so impatient. I'll take them off
myself,' she said.

My physical strength suddenly drained away and I stood
there like a piece of wood as I thought of Zhao Yue. On our

first night together, she had gripped my neck tight, asking me, 'Do you love me? Do you love me?'

'Put on your clothes and go home,' I said.

Young Lover was struck dumb by this. She looked embarrassed. 'Have I made you angry? Please forgive me. I'm young, I don't understand a lot.'

'It's nothing to do with you,' I said. 'I'm going back to Chengdu.'

CHAPTER TWENTY-FIVE

Twenty Volkswagen Passats drove into the precinct court-yard. In line with Bighead's requirements, every car had been spray-painted blue and equipped with the best police lights and sirens. The anti-smear windscreens and external trimmings were flawless. Bighead looked delighted. At the same time, however, he was shouting at his minions to check all the cars, and even blustered to me, 'If there's anything wrong with your cars, I'll send you to Pi County.'

Pi County was the biggest jail in Chengdu. I bowed obsequiously, just like they did to the Japanese army in old times.

'Of course I wouldn't dare,' I said.

Secretly I was thinking: Just see how I get my revenge on you later, you bastard.

We'd arranged to have dinner at the Workers' Café — my

idea. The owner was a celebrity in local cultural circles who Li Liang had admired for a long time.

In Chengdu you come across a lot of these so-called celebrities. Li Liang was always bragging that he'd drunk tea with this poet or eaten with that artist. As a supposed man of culture, I'd try to sound politely impressed. But Bighead had zero patience and inevitably poured cold water on Li Liang's enthusiasm.

'You paid the bill, I suppose? How much? Seven hundred? Fuck, couldn't you have used that money to buy us some booze?'

I'd laugh. Li Liang would glare and say that Bighead was a blockhead who only knew how to stuff his face. His very existence was an insult to the cultured and refined.

The dinner was a chance for Li Liang to meet the owner, and thus a reason for him to come out with us. Drug addict Li Liang lived a regular life. Every day he stayed home drinking tea, reading, playing computer games and getting a fix every couple of hours. He looked calmly indifferent to everything. Bighead and I had ceased trying to persuade him to stop shooting up. That day at his place we'd gone on at him for ages but he still wouldn't agree to go to the rehab centre. His nose was running as he looked everywhere for needles. Half an hour later he emerged from the bedroom and told us, 'You don't understand this. Just get out.'

Li Liang had lost weight. His face was pale, but he was in quite good spirits. He'd quit drinking and didn't talk much, spending most of the night listening to Bighead and me talking business. It wasn't until the patron came over to say hello that he showed some life, and they chatted for a while about the current state of Chengdu's arts scene. Bighead pretended to snore. However, we hadn't finished eating before Li Liang himself yawned massively and a big stream of snot ran down to his mouth. His eyes were glazed.

'Is something up?' I asked him.

He didn't answer. Swaying slightly, he picked up his leather bag and made his way towards the bathroom. Bighead gave me a look. My heart sank, and I chewed my chopsticks as I thought, Li Liang is finished.

I remembered an incident in 1994, when Li Liang and I were returning to Chengdu by train, and came across two farm labourers also going back to Sichuan. They were dark, dirty and strong and had taken our seats, where they were cracking watermelon seeds and making a mess everywhere. I asked them to return our seats and they didn't listen, just started cursing me. I was furious, and took out the Mongolian knife Bighead had given me. Li Liang said the expression on my face was terrifying. When those guys saw it, they guessed I wasn't easily bullied and left resentfully. When we sat down, I told Li Liang what I'd learnt from this response: It was better to be beaten to death than scared to death.

He said, 'It doesn't really matter whether you're scared to death or beaten to death. It's still death at the hands of others. A true man should be able to control his death. Being killed can't compare with committing suicide.'

Looking at his shaking back in the restaurant, I felt sick. How would I judge him if he were to die now?

The next time I saw Bighead Wang he casually mentioned the fleet of cars I'd helped him buy. I realised what he was after and handed him an envelope. Inside was 14,000 yuan. Bighead took a quick look round, then grabbed the envelope with amazing speed and put it into his bag as if he was a thief. His face bloomed like a flower and he stared at me with almost religious devotion. Actually, the whole business had gone quite smoothly. Twenty cars with a mark-up of 1700 each. After Bighead's cut, I still had 20,000 left.

I'd made a big show of wanting to split this with my sister, but she'd told me, 'It's enough for me if you sort out your own life and don't give Mum and Dad any more cause to worry about you.'

My nephew Dudu chimed in. 'Uncle is a bad boy. He always gets Grandma mad.'

My face felt hot and I slapped him.

Last week I'd told my mother that I wanted to move out. She was upset, but silently packed my stuff for me. I guiltily explained that I was so busy that I had to work overtime every day and that was why I wanted to live closer to work.

She sighed, 'You're big enough to make your own decisions. As long as everything goes smoothly, that's OK.'

When I walked out through the yard, I saw the old lady

on the balcony, crying as she looked down at me. It made me sad.

When I failed my university entrance exams the first time round, the old man was furious. He cursed me, saying that I only knew how to fool around. He even compared me with Uncle Wang's son.

'Look at Wang Dong! The same school, the same age as you. How come he can get accepted by Beijing University?'

I was already depressed, and flew into a rage on hearing this. I brought up the subject of genetics.

'Why don't you add that Uncle Wang is a deputy department chief? If I've amounted to nothing, it's down to you!'

His eyes blazed and he gave me a resounding slap. My mother caught his hand, which was poised to repeat the blow, and condemned his use of force. It would have been OK if she hadn't said anything, but when she did it fanned my feelings of being wronged. I opened the door and ran away, determined never to return. I was seventeen and didn't know anything about life, about what it meant to have a home. Ten years later, I'd come to understand this, but once again I was walking out.

The place I'd rented was empty. There was no TV, no stereo, just a big bed. I didn't go home at night till it was really late. Sometimes I thought 'home' was just a place you slept. Scholars and poets had said it was a haven or a nest where you could lick your wounds. That was a load of bullshit. The person who you slept with could betray you at any time, but a bed would always be there. It was a constant, which you could lie on, rely on, loyal to the end.

My window faced the street, and every morning I woke early because of the noise of the cars outside. People from outside the city came to Chengdu with their hopes and dreams, while I, a native son, lived out my nightmares to the sound of their footsteps.

On the bus home from the Chongqing business trip, I called Zhao Yue's mobile. She asked what I wanted.

'I miss you,' I said. 'Can I come home to see you?'

She refused and sounded uncomfortable. It seemed it wasn't convenient for her to talk right then.

I asked jealously, 'Is Yang Tao with you now?'

She was silent for nearly half a minute, then hung up. I dialled again but was told: *The phone you dialled is turned off. Please call later.*

I felt empty and staggered into the bus toilet where I stared with abhorrence at my old and ugly reflection in the mirror, just like a piece of rag. At that moment, the bus made a sharp turn, and sent me slamming into the wall. Zhao Yue's words rang in my ears: 'Rubbish! You're just rubbish!'

Emerging from the bathroom after washing my face, I flirted with the attendant.

'You're so beautiful,' I told her.

She gave a scornful smile and ordered me back to my seat.

'We'll arrive in Chengdu soon. Go home and tell your wife that.'

I said that my wife had died a long time ago. The other people on the bus raised their heads and stared at me.

I was tired of this city, weary of its pretensions. After leaving the Workers' Café, Bighead and I saw Li Liang home and then sat by the river for a while. We talked about times past. I said I'd probably leave in a few months since my boss wanted to transfer me to Shanghai. Bighead frowned and kept smoking. The Funan River, outlined by a few sparse lights, made a turn beside us, flowing silently to the east. All Chengdu people viewed the river as their mother; it carried their happiness and sorrows, partings and reunions. The laughter and tears of millions of Chen Zhongs and Zhao Yues merged here, flowing to the ocean, mighty and powerful, erasing everything.

Bighead stamped out his cigarette. 'It's late, let's go. If I don't go home now, Zhang Lan Lan will take sleeping pills again.'

Last October, I'd invited Bighead when I accompanied some clients to the Yellow Dragon resort. He was having some difficulties with his wife at that time. He left work without telling her he was going out and was even audacious enough to turn off his mobile. At the resort we had a big gambling session and Bighead won more than 17,000 yuan. He was in an ebullient mood and took a woman to his room that night. Their lovemaking was as loud as the thunder of guns and could probably be heard miles away. Wang Yu from Neijiang admired it a lot. 'Your classmate has so much energy' he said. 'The building has almost been demolished by his fucking.'

When Bighead went home, however, Zhang Lan Lan was suspicious. Perhaps he didn't pay her his usual attentions. Apparently she interrogated him with the aid of some specialist police appliances including an electric baton. Bighead fought back however, and handcuffed her to the bed for three hours. After she got free, Bighead's wife took a lot of sleeping pills. She left a will that cursed her husband's ancestors, and said, *I will haunt you even when I become a ghost.*

I didn't dare to visit his home for a couple of months after that.

Handing Bighead another Zhonghua cigarette, I said, 'Screw you. I was asking for your advice. Can you at least pretend to give a fuck?'

He lit the cigarette and thought.

'Will it be any different if you go to Shanghai? It's not about where you are. You won't be happy until you do something about your dog-farting temper.'

After a pause, he looked at me intently and then said, 'Do you know why I've never liked Zhao Yue?'

Why?

He raised his voice and said, 'Since you two are divorced, I may as well tell you everything. I once caught her doing it with another man.'

My jaw dropped but no words would come out.

Bighead tossed away his cigarette and added, 'She even said that if I didn't tell you, I could do anything I liked with her.'

CHAPTER TWENTY-SIX

I called Zhao Yue and told her I was leaving for Shanghai. There was stunned silence, as if she didn't know what to say. Finally she lashed out: 'So when are you coming back?'

She sounded upset. My heart skipped a beat as I remembered how at her graduation she'd embraced me and said, 'Even if you don't want me, I still want to go to Chengdu and be with you!'

For a brief moment I felt like abandoning my plan. But then I remembered Bighead's words and my heart became as hard as a stone.

'What's left in Chengdu for me?' I said. 'If I go, I don't plan to return.'

Zhao Yue started crying. Softly putting down the receiver, I studied the cruel smile on my face in the mirror.

Bighead Wang had said that the guy was called Yang Tao. The incident had occurred last December, while I'd been doing some company training in Nanjing. Bighead said they didn't have a stitch on, and hadn't even locked the door. Zhao Yue had remained calm, whereas Yang Tao was paralysed by shock. Bighead said he'd wanted to kill Yang Tao, but a completely naked Zhao Yue had restrained him, not letting him land a blow. According to Bighead, Zhao Yue had acted like a cheap whore, from start to finish, not seeming embarrassed at all. Apparently Zhao Yue went looking for Bighead afterwards, and tearfully promised that she'd never do it again and would be faithful to me from now on. Bighead said that any time he brought up Zhao Yue I got mad, so he didn't dare tell me.

He kept his head down. Meanwhile, I was shaking violently, my mind racing. Finally I kicked him in the stomach with one foot and pushed him to the ground like a piece of meat. My eyes were red. Punching his nose, I told him, 'Screw you! If I ever consider you as a friend again I'm not a human being!'

That evening I decided to get my revenge. Deceit was like a sheathed knife: when the truth came out, it always hurt people. I had to make Zhao Yue pay a proper price, pay for everything. Otherwise, I thought, what's the point of me still being alive?

I had 60,000 or so in savings; the 50,000 Old Lai in Chonqing had promised me hadn't trickled into my account yet. But there was still enough money to pay for a hit on Yang Tao. In high school I had a classmate called

Liang Dagang who'd done a few years in the army. After-wards, he worked as a bodyguard for a pawnbroker and car racketeer dealing mostly in stolen goods; around half of the stolen cars in Chengdu passed through his hands. Liang Dagang opened his own company last year, to collect debts on people's behalf. It was said that he already had one death on his conscience. I'd bumped into him recently in Ran Fang Street and sat with him a while. He said he wanted to underwrite all our company's debts — to give us protection in the case of any legal difficulties.

He let his jacket fall open slightly and at his waist I glimpsed the muted glint of a gun.

I'd told Zhao Yue that I was off in a fortnight. If I wasn't wrong, she'd be worrying now about our property. After our divorce we'd agreed that the apartment would go to her but all the contracts were in my name. Zhao Yue was one for details: there was no way she'd let me leave with things still like that. Whatever show of emotion she'd put on, it was definitely fake, and I vowed to myself that from now on I'd never believe her tears. My calculation was that she'd be concerned that I was planning to go back on my word and try to take the apartment.

Shortly before our wedding, we'd argued about a pre-nuptial agreement. Everything had gone smoothly until then. We'd just been to the Golden Bull hospital for our medical inspections. Zhao Yue's face was red as she told me the doctor had prodded her for ages, until she nearly wet herself. I guffawed, which made her a bit embarrassed, so I consoled her by saying, 'This is a good thing. No one wants us to break down in the middle of production.' And I made a rude gesture to show that I didn't mind displaying my equipment in front of the doctor.

She hit me. 'You're a complete bastard.'

At the marriage training class later that day, I whispered to her, 'We should do a pre-nup. How about it?'

Her face darkened and she accused me of bad faith. 'We haven't even got married yet and you're already thinking of throwing me over,' she said.

'You really are a peasant,' I told her. 'What does this have to do with divorcing or not? Modern people need to think modern.'

In spite of everyone else looking at us, Zhao Yue stormed out in a huff. 'Yes, I'm a peasant, so what? If there's anyone willing to sign a pre-nup with you, go and find her!'

My first instinct was to stay put, but I decided to think of the big picture and so forced myself to follow her. She went on at me for ages, furious, wounded and hurt, and I only saved the situation by reciting a parody of Xin Qiji's poem: *In front of a three-wheeled car/on a rubbish tip/Chengdu drifter/get out your cock/you're being sweet/ but she's still mad.*[19]

Zhao Yue smiled through her tears. 'If Xin Qiji knew while he was alive that you'd done such stupid things with his words, he'd have died of anger.'

Then she told me seriously, 'I refuse to go to lawyers. I agreed to be married to you for our whole lives.'

My heart jumped exquisitely and I embraced her thin waist.

A monk at Wenshu Temple had once said to me: 'See through things; everything is false!' Now I realised how stupid I was. Who made me so lacking in intelligence?

This time it was Zhao Yue who asked to see me. After work, I drove straight to the Fragrant Hotpot Restaurant in Xiyan district to meet her. Five months before I'd refused to go there when Zhao Yue asked me. Now it was too late, too late for everything.

'If I hadn't turned you down that day, do you think we'd still be together now?' I asked in a sentimental voice.

Zhao Yue lowered her head. 'Is there any point in asking that now?'

Her mouth trembled. It seemed she wanted to cry again.

I'd rehearsed my lines I didn't know how many times. Zhao Yue couldn't cope with other people's emotions. When we watched *Titanic*, long before anyone else she'd started to cry as though she was about to die. That was the first objective of my attack tonight: to get her emotional. I took a mouthful of beer and looked softly at her. Actually my heart was icing over and becoming hard like metal.

'Now that I'm going to Shanghai I don't know when I'll be back,' I told her. 'Perhaps I won't even be able to return for your and Yang Tao's wedding.'

Zhao Yue kept up her act. 'Yang Tao and I are just friends. Who says I'm going to marry him?'

I silently cursed, but managed to feign a happy expression.

'You mean I still have a chance?'

'You're going to Shanghai,' she said. 'How can you look after me?'

Now we'd got to the main topic. I fixed her with a sorrowful look.

'I'll always wait for you,' I said. 'It doesn't matter where you are, whether or not you're married, I'll wait. I'll use the rest of my life to make up for my mistake.'

My tone was as solemn and respectful as at a funeral. Zhao Yue's eyes gradually filled with tears.

Buttering people up was one of my great strengths. It was also one of my greatest weapons in seducing women. At school when I was chasing the school beauty, Cheng Jiao, many of my competitors were taller, more handsome and richer than me. In the end though, I won her. The first time I got her clothes off, my bedroom skills were still raw. She had to show me the ropes, sighing, 'I've been deceived by your fearless gob.'

Zhao Yue was even shallower than Cheng Jiao, I thought, because she didn't know who she had feelings for. It was easy to move her. All the same, I felt an ache as I realised how well I knew her.

The restaurant was very efficient. At precisely seven thirty they played Zhang Ai Jia's 'The Price of Love':

Do you still remember the dreams of youth?
Like a bunch of flowers never fading.
Stay with me through the wind and showers.
Watch the changing world.

This was our song. At a New Year's party in 1994, I'd worn a black suit and Zhao Yue a white skirt and red top. We linked hands and passionately led the singing, to the approval of everyone there. When Zhao Yue heard the song, her lips trembled. I looked straight into her eyes and sang softly: *That deep love always in my heart, even though you have gone.*

I gripped her hand gently and said I didn't know when I'd get another chance to sing the song with her. I hadn't finished speaking before Zhao Yue was in tears. Her chopsticks fell to the table.

I shook my head and said that my biggest regret in life was letting her go. 'You gave me your best few years,' I told her, 'but I let you down. I didn't even buy you any decent clothes.'

Zhao Yue threw herself into my arms, cried bitterly. People looked at us. I cradled Zhao Yue's head to my chest and waved at them, smiling.

When we'd finished eating Zhao Yue's eyes were still wet. I felt my heart soften a bit and asked her: 'Do you think we can get back together? Be like before?'

Zhao Yue said there was no way she could forget the scene in our apartment that day. 'You hurt me too much!'

I thought gloomily that she was a cheap bitch. I'd given her a chance but she hadn't taken it.

My plan was to suggest to Zhao Yue that we spend the night together. I was about to leave Chengdu and it could be the last time we were together in this world. It was also the seventh anniversary of our first kiss in that campus grove on 17 August 1994. We'd told each other how we felt. The moonlight was very strong, making her body smooth and clear as jade. 'My Zhao Yue really is as beautiful as a goddess,' I'd said.

She'd poured herself shyly into my embrace, wrapped her arms around me so tightly I could hardly breathe. Each year we'd celebrated that day. Zhao Yue said that it was more important than our wedding. Marriage was just a form, but love, that was happiness. In two days time it would be exactly seven years. That was 2555 days and nights. Fuck, even I couldn't help getting emotional. To begin with Zhao Yue said no to my suggestion of a last night together, but when she saw my tears — although no doubt the apartment crossed her mind as well — she finally agreed.

The Golden Bay Hotel was an establishment where our company often put up clients. I'd already arranged everything. When we went into the room I let down her hair, and caressed and stroked it as I'd done many times before. Zhao Yue nestled in my arms, a little shy. When all her clothes were off, I kissed her.

'It's been months since I kissed you,' I said.

Zhao Yue looked at me with deep sadness. This expression triggered a lot of memories in me. In the winter vacation of our third college year, she'd seen me off at the railway station. After my graduation she came again to the station to see me off and embraced me, crying so loudly the rail staff couldn't bear to watch. On the day of our divorce, before we set out from home she straightened my tie and told me to take care.

Suddenly I thought I couldn't go through with it. A voice inside me was saying, *Everyone makes mistakes. Forgive her.*

I looked away as I blinked back tears. Very seriously I asked her, 'Can you tell me about you and Yang Tao?'

She got up angrily, and said she was leaving.

'There's really nothing between us, nothing at all. Do you think everyone is like you?'

I shut my eyes, feeling as if I'd been drenched with cold water. Then I sighed and said that I was in the wrong.

'I shouldn't bring that up right now.'

I pulled her to me.

Do you still remember the dreams of youth?
Like a bunch of flowers never fading.
Stay with me through the wind and showers.
Watch the changing world.

The price that we pay for love is hard to forget.
That deep love always in my heart,
Even though you have gone.

Move on; people always want to improve themselves.
Move on; it's hard to avoid suffering and struggle.

There was a knock at the door. Zhao Yue nudged me anxiously and said, 'There's someone outside.'

Caressing her face I said, 'So what? What are you afraid of? I'm here.'

She wasn't reassured and told me to go and look.

'We're not husband and wife any more,' she said.

I smiled. 'OK, whatever you say.'

Zhao Yue gave me a lovely smile, which was repaid with an equally charming look. Zipping up, I went and opened the door. Yang Tao stood there, looking enraged, in a red T-shirt. I patted his shoulder, buckled my belt and said, 'Go in. Your girlfriend is already naked and waiting for you.'

CHAPTER TWENTY-SEVEN

Every autumn the skin on my hands peeled. Western doctors blamed a vitamin deficiency; Chinese doctors said that it was too much heat in my blood. Zhao Yue claimed that I had been a snake in my past life. Had I watched all this distantly from a remote cave in the mountains?: love and hate, sorrow and happiness. Would this life that was a compound of hundreds of accumulated lives be like the skin on my hands, flaking away bit by bit in the cold autumn?

Autumn 2001 in Chengdu was little different from the autumns of past years. Yellow leaves were everywhere; the wind blew sand into eyes. Each night people died, and those keeping vigil over the bodies played mahjong, their faces alive with pleasure. Babies were born, their umbilical cords cut and their fates set. Li Liang said,

'You'd better believe it. Life's a joke played on us by God.'

I laughed as I left the Golden Bay Hotel. The girl on reception said goodbye and I gave her a graceful half bow.

'Thanks for making that call,' I said.

Zhao Yue should be feeling thoroughly humiliated. I wondered whether Yang Tao would just climb on her and carry on where I'd left off. The stove was hot and so Zhao Yue shouldn't mind frying one more dish. I reckoned that a guy who'd stepped into someone else's shoes wouldn't say no to sloppy seconds. The only pity was that I'd had to pay the 300 yuan room fee in advance. I reminded myself to get a receipt.

The two of us had settled our accounts; we were even. I shook my fist at the sky. This evening, that woman called Zhao Yue was struck from my ledger. We'd spent seven years establishing a truth: love was no more than a by-product of sexual excitement. Or to put it more simply: in this world there was no such thing as love. Deceit and betrayal were all.

In a daze, I jumped in the car and sped off. Suddenly a taxi screeched to a halt by my side. The driver stuck out his head and cursed me furiously.

'You want to die! Blockhead, can't you drive a car?'

I apologised, but his anger didn't abate and he went on cursing for ages. I smiled, thinking that this was what came of forgiveness. If I'd got out and smacked him in the face, the son of a bitch wouldn't even have dared to fart.

After drinking so much, my bladder was swollen. I

stopped my car on the second ring-road and undid my fly. In the dusky lamplight, the patch of grass appeared to be withering. When were my green years? Thanks to my nutricious piss, this grass should grow well next year, but where would I find nourishment?

A long-distance bus whistled past, several faces glued to the window watching as I let forth a torrent. Just as I was losing all inhibition, I heard a woman call out from somewhere behind me, 'You're shameless, pissing on the street.'

I was embarrased and quickly put away the instrument of my disgrace. When I turned my head, I saw a shadow approaching.

I believed that in this world there were no truly honourable people. Given the right combination of time, place and person, anyone would cheat—even an impotent guy or a frigid woman—if they thought they could get away with it.

Zhao Yue had disputed this, but with one sentence I'd forced her into a corner. 'If you and Louis Koo were alone in a room and he tried to seduce you, would you resist or not?'

Hong Kong film star Louis Koo was her idol. Zhao Yue tried to avoid answering, but finally was only able to come up with the response that there was no way such a situation would ever occur. I'd dropped the subject, thinking that this basically said it all about so-called true love.

Approaching me through the dark was a girl of about twenty-six or twenty-seven. Her face was made up like a fried breadcake. She was wearing shorts and a skimpy top which revealed her belly button. Just from one glance I could tell she was a hooker. I turned to get in the car, but she stopped me.

'Hey, handsome, give me a bit of business. One hundred yuan will do.'

I was about to tell her to scram, when suddenly I had a thought.

'Will you do it with your mouth?'

She shot a disdainful look at what I'd just put away and spat on the ground. 'With the mouth it will be 500.'

Sneering, I shut the car door and started the engine. The desperate girl threw herself against the window, continuing to haggle.

'Four hundred! Three hundred!'

Zhou Weidong always eulogised about what he referred to as a Lewinsky. Once he told me he wanted to open a club on the river called the White House Kiss. When I went home and told Zhao Yue about this, she muttered, 'That Zhou Weidong really is an animal.'

To win her favour, I'd immediately drawn a line between Zhou Weidong and myself, saying, 'Exactly. He's undermining conjugal love between a man and wife, it's degrading. But in our case … '

Zhao Yue gave me a look. 'I know what your dirty idea is. Forget it.'

At that moment I felt like a mouse in a trap.

On the road, the lights of a stream of cars approached and then faded into the night. The night market had already shut down; the vendors had put away their pots, pans, dippers and basins. Their faces expressive of hardship and loss, they were heading back to their homes. Every night people on the street thought about going home, but who waited for me? Who was missing me?

The girl practised her oral kung fu on me, her long hair floating over my waist. All that was solid melted and, as the world soundlessly collapsed, memories rolled over me.

In the autumn of 1996, on Mount Emei, I'd wrapped an overcoat around Zhao Yue's body but she'd continued to shiver, her teeth chattering like a horse's hooves on flagstones.

'Twenty years on, if we come here again we can't go back on our promise,' she said.

'By that time you'll be an old woman,' I replied. 'I'll want a newer model.'

Zhao Yue had kicked my leg, hit my chest with her fist and chased me furiously, almost beating me into pulp. Finally I embraced her. She struggled but couldn't get free and all at once calmed down. I kissed her gently, then we turned our heads and saw a vast expanse of white clouds. A red sun slowly rose, bringing the day, illuminating our bodies with a golden glow.

In 1998, when we departed from the North-East, Zhao Yue and her mother wept on each other's shoulders at the train station. My mother-in-law took my hand and said, 'Chen Zhong, Zhao Yue hasn't had many good times in her life. You should treat her well.'

Zhao Yue sobbed so much she nearly put her back out. I put my arm around her shoulders and earnestly promised her mother, 'Don't worry, I'll be good to her.'

As the train went through Shanhaiguan, Zhao Yue asked, 'Did you mean what you said?'

I answered indistinctly with my mouth full. 'If I cheat on you, I am a dog.'

She didn't pick up on the dark note in my voice, and smiled like a flower blossoming.

That mouth-artist had gone. I started to doubt my memories: those fragments - true or false? In this city tomb, who could serve as a reliable witness to my youth? Li Liang once said, 'You can live for many people, but you can only die for one.' But now, this night, who was I living for? Who could I die for? I zipped up and threw myself into the front seat. Starting the car, I spun the steering wheel and did a U-turn. The car door scraped against a tree with a soul-piercing sound.

Zhao Yue's boyfriend before me was called Ren Li Hua—a name that made it hard to guess whether its owner was a man or a woman. After that business in the woods, Zhao Yue never spoke about him, no matter what. She kept her trap shut and, on pain of death, refused to divulge any details of their relationship.

'I've seen it all anyway,' I said. 'What's left to be embarrassed about?'

Even as I spoke, I was unsure what I actually wanted to know, but the more she refused to tell me, the more I felt there was something wrong. We had a massive argument. At one point I couldn't control my temper and said nastily, 'You checked to see that Ren Li Hua's cock wasn't up to much before you came looking for me!'

She went mad, and stormed into the kitchen and grabbed a knife. She brandished it, saying she wanted to stab me. I made her hand it over but still she bit and kicked at me. Tears streamed down her face as she screamed, 'Chen Zhong, you have lost all goodness. You'll come to a bad end.'

There was a lot of stuff about Zhao Yue that I'd never know now. It was widely rumoured at university that she'd attempted to commit suicide because of what happened in the woods. I raised the subject a few times, but she always denied it, and if I pressed her she got tetchy. Last year on Christmas Eve, however, we were embracing tenderly, with her face pressed to my chest.

'I'll never commit suicide for another person,' she said. 'If I die, I want to die for you.'

She'd hardly finished speaking when the Christmas bells started in the distance and we heard thunderous cheers from the bar downstairs.

I was suddenly full of a nameless dread. Surely Zhao Yue wouldn't commit suicide?

A taxi drove by. The road light at my side winked twice

and then, without a sound, it went out. My mind suddenly threw up this thought: a person's death was like a light going out! My brain felt as if it'd been struck by lightning. Dancing spots before my eyes that gradually formed into Zhao Yue's face.

Room 308 in the Golden Bay Hotel. The door was still unlocked. I grabbed the handle, my heart leaping madly. After waiting two seconds to cool down, I gently pushed open the door.

No one. The place was as silent and still as the grave. The TV was on, the sound turned down; a few shadows with happy faces danced across the screen. Their lips moved but I didn't know what they were saying. All the lights were on, the sheets tangled on the bed. The paper I'd used to clean my shoes stuck up from the edge of the wastepaper basket, fluttering in a slight draught.

CHAPTER TWENTY-EIGHT

There'd been no follow-up to my interview with the big boss. Fatty Dong continued to act as general manager, his stomach stuck out in front and his arse protruding behind. His manner was increasingly high-handed and he often produced enough saliva to drown people. Zhou Weidong summarised his three favourite sayings as follows:

1. You're wrong!
2. I can't just sign this.
3. You can disagree, but you still have to obey.

He imitated Fatty Dong, thrusting out his stomach as he walked around.

'Chen Zhong, do you dare disobey?' he said in Fatty Dong's blustering tone.

I beat the desk and laughed loudly.

'Genius. You've got him down to a T.'

I'd had a very tough time over the past two months. Disregarding Head Office's instructions, Fatty Dong asked accounts to deduct 5000 yuan from my salary each month. As it was the slowest season for sales, I was making less than 3000 yuan a month. If I hadn't had some capital to fall back on, I would have had to declare bankruptcy. Last week at the Binjiang Hotel I'd seen Zegna suits on sale, the cheapest going for just 4600. I hesitated for a long time before deciding to pass it up. I was almost thirty years old, life wasn't forever, and it was time to think about the future.

In my university essays, I loved using the word 'lifetime'. A 'lifetime' of true love, a 'lifetime's' ambition, blah blah blah. Back then I'd genuinely believed there were lots of things that were essentially unchanging. It was only now that I realised, apart from the food you ate, nothing else was fixed. That which you valued most would eventually turn to shit.

I called the HR director, Mr Liu, and asked him whether there were any new arrangements forthcoming for the Sichuan branch. Disappointingly his voice held no trace of his former warmth, and he said that first I should concentrate on doing a good job in my current position. I wondered what the problem was. Whatever it was, I was sure Fatty Dong had something to do with it. The jerk had paid his own expenses for a trip to Head Office in August. Since returning he had been abnormally energetic. He stuck his nose into all of the sales team's business, big and small. He even rejected my proposal for firing Liu Three. I criticised Liu's lack of ability, and said that Old Lai from Chongqing wasn't happy with him.

Fatty Dong waved his pipe like a big shot and said, 'I decide how to make use of people. You can disagree but you still have to obey.'

I was desperate to beat this piece of dog shit, but Zhou Weidong dragged me away.

I also still hadn't got that 50,000 that Old Lai from Chongqing owed me. When I called to rebuke him for not keeping his promise, he joked, 'You're putting so much pressure on me. All my savings are tied up in this. Can you give me a bit more time? I'll send the money to you personally after I've got the goods off my hands.'

I almost swore at him. Your fucking assets are worth millions but you can't find a piffling 50,000 yuan? I thought. Do you really take me for such an idiot?

This didn't look good. This guy was notoriously devious, and it was quite possible he was thinking up some wicked plan. Fortunately I'd prudently kept all the relevant receipts. Even if he shrugged off the money he owed me, he couldn't do the same with the money he owed the company.

The work situation disheartened me though. I could tell from Boss Liu's tone there was little hope of promotion. Even if they kept deducting 5000 yuan every month, I guessed I'd still be in debt by the time Taiwan returned to the motherland. When I discussed this with Zhou

Weidong, he urged me to change jobs.

'Your debts are a civil case at most,' he said. 'So you don't have any criminal liability.'

The guy always bragged that he was an elite graduate of the China University of Political Science and Law, but his graduation certificate had looked dodgy. Also, he without doubt had a vested interest in my future: it might have occurred to him that when I left it would create an opportunity for him. Last week he'd brought me some expense forms to sign and a cursory glance told there was something wrong with them. When I raised the matter, his face darkened and he said, 'Don't you do your expenses the same way?'

Without another word, I signed my name, thinking, Is there such a thing as an honest person anywhere?

Whatever happened, I had to stick it out until the end of the year. The year-end double salary bonus and annual commissions would be more than 20,000 yuan, which was worth having. Then in October there was our winter sales fair. As I was in charge of sales policy, it would be a good chance to boost my income. If I left now, it would be a waste. I'd had bad luck in everything this year, but I hoped that if I could just get through these next few months then everything would be better next year.

My mother had asked someone to tell my fortune, and was told that twenty-nine would be my glory year. I would get a big promotion and enjoy such success in business that money would flow to me like water. I wouldn't even have to do much, it would just be like picking up a wallet from the ground. After hearing this, I closed my door and laughed until I cried. Life; if there was no hope, where would we find the strength to live?

My mother was still freaking out about the apartment situation. She kept on at me to get justice for myself. I didn't know what to feel. 'Mother, give me a break, OK? Think of it as money spent because of an illness.'

She glared at me, then took out her temper on radishes and cabbages. I thought it was a good thing I hadn't told her about Zhao Yue's affair or the old lady would probably have gone and killed her. My mother had kept up her kung fu all these years and was a master of many disciplines. She was accomplished at Tai Ji swordplay, and I doubted Zhao Yue would last more than a few bouts with her.

That day when I went back to the Golden Bay Hotel in the hope of finding Zhao Yu and Yang Tao, I ended up driving around the Xiyan district until I was almost out of gas. Finally I returned to the Golden Bay and asked about them. The girl on the front desk said that she'd seen a woman and man walking out together but didn't notice their expressions. The woman had her head down, and the man was touching her in a sleazy way. On hearing that, I felt rather strange, as if grass was growing in my head. I stubbed out my cigarette, went back to my car and slapped myself hard. When all I could see was stars, I thought: Does tonight make me a winner or a loser?

◎ ◎ ◎

Bighead Wang and Li Liang both received invitations to Zhao Yue and Yang Tao's wedding.

Bighead Wang swore loyalty to me, saying that he wouldn't go. 'I'd rather wipe my ass with that money.'

Li Liang said that firstly Bighead's suggestion was mean, and secondly it would result in lead poisoning.

After consulting me, Li Liang went along as Chen Zhong's official delegate, to congratulate them and deliver a gift of 600 yuan in a red envelope.

Apparently the wedding was a big do with lots of guests lined up to congratulate them. They'd even invited the main anchor of Chengdu TV station. Zhao Yue's wedding dress was said to be ravishing, and she smiled like a flower. Apparently she refused several toasts on Yang Tao's behalf, and someone joked that she was afraid that he'd get too drunk to perform on their wedding night.

Zhao Yue put her head on Yang's shoulder and smiled. 'Of course,' she said.

'I couldn't watch any more,' Li Liang said. 'When I left, no one noticed. To be honest, we were wrong. Zhao Yue is actually tougher than you.'

I was in Neijiang that day. Li Liang called me straight afterwards, to give me a rundown of the wedding. I listened to him while continuing to eat and drink with my client, Wang Yu, who was moaning about the company's rigid systems and low efficiency. When I shot him a fierce look he shut up immediately, as if I'd flicked a switch.

Turning away from him, I said softly to Li Liang,

'Did you congratulate her for me and wish her a happy marriage?'

Li Liang was silent for a while, then said, 'Don't think too much about things. This is just life.'

I laughed. 'Fuck you. Would it have killed you to say a few words for me?'

My hands had started to tremble uncontrollably. My glass dropped and smashed into pieces on the ground, splashing wine onto my shoes, which shimmered under the light.

My spirits revived, however, after polishing off two bottles of spirits. The ceiling seemed to be shaking far above me, and the world was brilliantly colourful. Wang Yu's face was sometimes close and sometimes distant. His mouth opened and shut and I wondered what the hell he was talking about. Suddenly I laughed and hit the table. Everyone turned around and glared at me.

'What the fuck are you smiling about?' Wang Yu said. 'What's made you so happy?'

I laughed until my tears flowed.

'My wife is getting married today. Let's have one more drink for her.'

He shook his head. 'You've had too much, kid. You're full of shit.'

When I raised my glass again, I slid to the ground. My head hit the table edge and I saw stars. Wang Yu hurriedly came round to help me up.

'Are you OK?' he asked.

I kicked and lashed out.

'Fuck it! Fuck you! You're all bastards.'

Outside the restaurant: a young smartly dressed guy sat on the ground weeping uncontrollably. Passers-by stopped and pointed at him, laughing.

On the other side of town: a couple of newly-weds got into a wedding car and to the cheers of their friends, slowly drove away towards their happy, warm new home.

'Why did you marry Zhao Yue?' my sister's husband had once asked me.

'I love her.'

'What? I can't hear. Speak up!'

I'd grabbed the microphone and shouted, 'I love her!'

All the guests began to laugh, whistle and applaud. Zhao Yue held my hand, and blushed as she looked at me. Tears shone in her eyes.

That was 18 June 1998, my wedding day. My long, long-ago wedding.

The third day after I got back from Neijiang, Bighead called and asked me to hurry to his office straight away. I'd been asleep; looking at my watch I saw it was 3 a.m. Furious, I told him to fuck off. Just as I was about to hang up, he shouted, 'It's Li Liang. Quick! He's in trouble.'

I'd asked Li Liang before where he got his gear. He always dodged this question, and if I asked again, his eyes would flare dangerously.

'Why do you want to know? Are you going to inform on me?'

I reluctantly let it drop, denouncing Li Liang's lack of scruples and inability to tell when someone was doing him a favour.

Even if he didn't tell me, I could guess. The two main centres for heroin dealing in Chengdu were Wannianchang in the east and Sima Bridge in the north. Most Chengdu powder brothers went to Sima Bridge to score. Recently the police had busted a lot of dealers there. After my brother-in-law published the news, he repeatedly asked me to urge Li Liang to be careful.

'It's too dangerous,' he said. 'He should quit.'

When I told Li Liang, he just sneered, looking at me coldly in the way that triad gangsters look at chopper fodder.

By the time I reached the station, he was crouched trembling in a corner. He was barefoot with his hands cuffed behind his back, and his face was blue and green with bruises. There was blood at the corners of his mouth. His shirt was ripped to shreds, his pale scrawny chest exposed When he saw me, he turned away quickly, his shoulders shaking. He seemed ashamed. I felt sad for him, and draped my jacket over his shoulders.

'Don't worry, Bighead and I are here,' I said. 'You'll be OK.'

Bighead said that Li Liang had been unlucky. He'd just scored when the police arrived and threw him to the ground, and he might have suffered a blow to the head.

Struggling to free himself, he'd seized hold of the arresting officer's balls. By the time he let go, the cop's face had turned purple. In fact he was still lying in a room next door crying. Bighead said that if he hadn't arrived, Li Liang would have been severely beaten. I asked what we should do. Bighead shrugged.

'What else can we do? We have to spend some money. We need to get him out of here tonight. It'll be too difficult tomorrow.'

I asked how much. He sighed and extended four plump fingers and a thumb. I took a deep breath. 'That much?'

His expression became serious. 'Fifty thousand may not be enough. Do you know how much stuff Li Liang had on him? One hundred grams. That's ten years at least!'

I nearly fainted.

'It's so late. Where can we go to get that kind of money?' I said.

Bighead took a look around, then shut the door and said in a low voice, 'We have a few days to get the money. I already talked this through with the chief. For the moment, we just need Li Liang to write a cheque.'

I noticed that Bighead Wang was dressed unusually formally. The badges on his hat and shoulder were shiny, the creases of his trousers sharp. It was different from his usual butt-cleavage image. For some reason I was suspicious. I smoked a cigarette as I studied him. My scrutiny obviously made Bighead uncomfortable. He took off his hat and slapped it on the desk.

'If I'm getting one fucking cent from Li Liang, I'm a son of bitch,' he swore.

I didn't believe in vows. Bighead Wang's words failed to satisfy me but they reminded me of something that had happened while we were at university.

In the second semester of our sophomore year, Big Brother and Bighead Wang had a fight over a 30 yuan gambling debt. Bighead brandished a mop, Big Brother wielded a chair. Both were heavyweight contestants and they fought at close quarters until the dormitory was nearly destroyed. My basin, bowl, mirror and bookstand were totally wrecked in that battle. After the fight, it was time for a battle of words. Separated by a desk, the two cursed each other furiously. Bighead Wang said that someone who didn't pay their debts should be fucked by donkeys. Big Brother almost went insane. He kicked the air several times, saying that he wanted to kill Bighead. Chen Chao and I had to use all our strength to restrain them and I guessed our arms were stretched several centimetres during the process. When Big Brother realised that he couldn't escape us despite his struggles, he cursed Bighead venomously: 'Fuck you! You would sell your own dad for one cent!'

After carrying Li Liang up to the third floor of his building, I was out of breath. I lay on his couch and couldn't get up. I hadn't realised it in the police station, but when I got him home I discovered he was quite badly hurt. There was blood all over his legs and his wrists were extremely swollen. He kept coughing.

I turned over every box and basket in the kitchen until finally I found some safflower oil. I rubbed the oil into his skin and at the same time shared my suspicions..

'Firstly, I haven't seen anyone else dealing with this case, and it was only Bighead who was talking about the money. Secondly, Bighead rarely wears a uniform, so how come he was dressed so formally tonight? Thirdly, he could have dealt with you himself. Why did he call me? What did he want me to witness?'

Li Liang frowned and took a deep breath, as if he was in great pain. Just as I was getting really worried, he pushed me away and said to the door: 'Come on in, Bighead. What are you standing out there for?'

CHAPTER TWENTY-NINE

Bighead Wang had been quite impressed by my kicking skills that day on the banks of the Funan River. Afterwards, he called me repeatedly, but every time I hung up without listening. Once he waited for me on my way home from work; he had a fawning smile. But by now I knew that concepts like 'friends' and 'brothers' were bullshit. The truth was, I could help him make money.

I didn't believe that Bighead had deliberately set out to trap Li Liang, but it was likely that he was taking advantage of Li Liang's misfortune to try and make himself a little profit. Joining the cops was the perfect way to corrupt a guy. Usually it took less than two years to become a poisonous bastard who would take a bite out of even their own father.

At high school I had a great friend by the name of Liu

Chunpeng. He used to steal watermelons from markets, and once we punctured a teacher's tyre together. When we both failed our university entrance exams, we stood in Hejiang Pavilion and sighed together, lamenting that heaven had turned a blind eye to us. Finally we wept on each other's shoulders. After high school graduation, he got a job as a cop on the railway station district beat. A few years later he'd become evil and didn't show anyone any favours. A friend of mine drove into some railings near the north train station; he was caught and told that his licence would be withdrawn. My friend asked me to plead for him. Liu Chunpeng said, 'OK, OK, your problem is my problem.'

Later however, he still fined my friend and took some points from his licence, which made me lose face. Another time I personally witnessed the guy beating a migrant worker until his face was bloody and he knelt and begged for mercy. It was all because the migrant worker had stepped on Liu Chunpeng's foot. After the beating, he was still mad and he kicked the worker's bag high into the air. A cup inscribed with the motto 'Serve the people' fell out, rolling and clattering down the street.

'You can trust Bighead, but you shouldn't trust any cop,' I told Li Liang.

'I already handed over the money,' Li Liang replied, 'so what's the point of talking about this?'

I continued to slander police's reputation, calling them beasts with badges. Li Liang looked me for a while then sighed and said, 'You know what your problem is? You don't take seriously the things you're supposed to take seriously, and you're way too serious about the things you should be relaxed about.'

Bighead's expression that day was ugly. Panting with rage, he puffed out his cheeks and glared at me. I was sure he'd heard what I'd said. I was uncomfortable; in fact, it was highly embarrassing. Just as I was about to say something, Li Liang went berserk. He dived into the bedroom and started to turn everything upside down, making a terrible noise. Bighead and I hurried after him and saw chests, cabinets and drawers already ransacked. He was out of breath and a strange sound came from his mouth.

'What are you looking for?' Bighead said. 'Don't worry, Chen Zhong and I will help you.'

Without turning his head, Li Liang said, 'There's one more packet! I still have one more. One more!' His voice was hoarse and grating, like a wolf howling in the wasteland.

Perhaps there was something wrong with Li Liang's memory. We turned the house upside down but didn't find the packet. By then his fits were getting more and more frightening. At one point he grabbed an empty needle and tried to stab it in his arm. Bighead and I threw ourselves on him and wrested back the needle, both of us sweating with the effort. Li Liang rolled and crawled on the floor, twisting his body in strange contortions like a worm. This was the first time I'd witnessed such a scene. I was shocked and uneasy, afraid that he'd have a heart attack and drop dead.

Bighead fought with him for a while, then wheezed out an order.

'Go and get a rope to tie him up!'

As I went to leave, Li Liang clung pathetically to my leg.

'Chen Zhong, I'm begging you! Go out and score for me!'

With a great effort I shook him off. He fell to the ground, his face covered with snot and tears, his lips blue and green. His pupils were dilated, like a corpse with open eyes.

We had to carry him downstairs on our shoulders. The sky was still dark and the whole city was deserted, except for a few people who had stayed up all night and floated past with ghostly expressions. When we stuffed Li Liang into the car, he shrieked loudly. The sound was as sharp as a knife, shaking my soul, making my guts shudder.

After a fifteen-day compulsory detox treatment, Li Liang had put on some weight. The day he came out of the clinic his manner was a bit weird. He had a strange smile, as if he was happy and disappointed at the same time. His facial muscles were twitching, so I guessed that maybe he was having withdrawal symptoms.

On the way home we stopped to eat at Liangjia Alley. Li Liang ate like a robot, chewing his rice expressionlessly and not saying a word.

I couldn't bear it any more and begged him, 'Bro, make some noise, OK? You're really scary like this.'

He poked at the slices of boiled pork in the bowl with his chopsticks, then said thoughtfully, 'Fuck, the restaurants outside the college gates had better food than this.'

On the second day after he disappeared, I dialled his

mobile repeatedly but he didn't answer. I went round to his place and almost hammered his door down, but there was no response. I felt an inexplicable fear. After hesitating a while, I summoned the courage to call Ye Mei. She asked me what I wanted.

'Go home and take a look,' I said. 'Li Liang might have killed himself.'

Li Liang's idol had always been Hai Zi, the poet. In 1989 Hai Zi committed suicide by lying on the railway tracks near Shanhaiguan. Li Liang claimed to have read all of his poetry. He'd come to the conclusion that Hai Zi's death made him a hero, and that those who clung to life should feel shamed by his example. Later, this became one of Li Liang's articles of faith. The second semester of our senior year, the literature society held a creative writing seminar where we pretentiously contemplated the future direction of Chinese literature. A group of vain young prats got so excited they had nosebleeds. When the meeting was about to end, Li Liang asked me, 'Chen Zhong, what do we live for?'

The students stared at me. I thought for a while and said, 'For happiness.'

Li Liang paced excitably denouncing my view.

'Wrong! Life has only one goal!'

That was 1994, and Li Liang was twenty-one. He was wearing a red striped T-shirt that he'd bought for 5 yuan at a small stand outside the campus. He didn't say what he thought the point of life was, but I knew anyway. It was death.

My happiness is a handful of dust
On a windless moonlit night the long grass suddenly
    trembled
Paper money floated and fell on the hills
Passers-by: your tears
Will surely erase the traces of my former lives
But those falling
Will also become more and more plentiful.
—Li Liang, 'Moonlit Night'

By the time Ye Mei dashed panting up the stairs, I'd lit my third cigarette. She didn't say a thing, just opened the door. Without removing my shoes I rushed in.

Li Liang wasn't there. His luxury apartment by the Funan River was as empty as a ransacked tomb. The window was wide open, the wind carrying the smell of rotten fish. A baby bird flew by and perched on a branch from which yellow leaves were falling. Autumn was here, and the bird was returning home.

After searching the whole house thoroughly, I had to concede that Li Liang's corpse wasn't concealed inside the wardrobe, under the bed or down the toilet. I'd even prodded the mattress all over, suspecting that he might have stitched himself inside. The whole time Ye Mei just stood there watching me race back and forth like a madman. Her eyes expresed contempt, as if I was a piece of dog shit and the sight of me might pollute her.

After I'd finished my search, she said coldly, 'I didn't know you were such a good friend of his.'

I was a bit mad, and answered sternly: 'Li Liang is my best friend in the world. He always will be! I would even …'

My face felt hot. Ye Mei had folded her arms and she had a look of complete disdain as she waited for me to finish. I mustered up my courage and said confidently, 'I would even die for him!'

She snorted and with a peculiarly savage expression said, 'Li Liang didn't really regard you as his friend. That 32,000 yuan you owe him—he's never forgotten about that.'

This was Ye Mei, a woman I was familiar with yet who was a stranger to me. In other words, what I was familiar with was just her body, or parts of her body. I'd never cared about her mind. That time when Li Liang had told me gloomily, she only listens to you now, I'd blushed and fled.

As a master in romance and whoring, I could vaguely sense how Ye Mei had felt about me that night in Leshan when she'd collapsed on top of my body letting out heart-rending cries. And when she'd thrown that glass of wine over me. What had confused me was her behaviour after-wards. From the day of her wedding up until today we'd met only six times and each time it was as if she'd just come out of the fridge. She gave me goose bumps.

After my divorce from Zhao Yue, she'd called me one morning at five o'clock. Confused, I asked who it was.

She said it was her.

Immediately I asked what was up.

She didn't reply.

Rubbing my eyes, I heard loud music coming down the phone line. After nearly a whole minute she suddenly said,

'Forget it. I dialled the wrong number, OK.'

Without another sound she hung up.

The sky was already a little light, a thread of dawn pen-etrating through the window into my sleepy eyes. I cradled the phone as I sat there stupidly, my mind empty. Later, I slept again and didn't wake until it was fully light. When I woke I felt a sense of loss, and wasn't sure whether it had been a dream.

I knew that what she said was true. Li Liang was totally different from me. I was careless and never knew how much money I had, let alone how much of that belonged to me and how much to others. I was the type of person who thought, there's 10 yuan in my wallet, so I'll spend 9 yuan on a pack of cigarettes. Li Liang was very meticulous: he remembered every favour he received and gave. But seeing as he remembered that I owed him 32,000, he should also remember what he owed me.

In our final semester at university, Li Liang was severely broke. All his money was lost at the mahjong table. He never won, but his addiction trumped that. Anytime some-one shouted in the corridor, we've got three but we're short one!, he'd be the first to dash out and sign up.

That semester I'd brought 2300 yuan with me, but blew it all within three months. At least half went on paying off Li Liang's gambling debt. He didn't even have enough money to buy his train ticket home to Chengdu, and depended on my generous support for everything. He had nowhere to stay when he got back to Chengdu, and so once again it was me who gave him a free room and board at my place. He smoked my father's Red Pagoda cigarettes, and my mother washed his socks.

Yes, that was it, my point. The value of friends lay in using each other. Those friendships where you'd die for each other might exist; on the other hand, they might just be fantasy.

So that afternoon, as the autumn leaves drifted in the dusty air, I looked for my drug ruined friend Li Liang. A white plastic bag sank slowly into the Funan River's grey and stinking water. I stood on the bank thinking, what 'life and death' friendships? Don't make me laugh.

CHAPTER THIRTY

There were two sorts of business trips in our company: 'profit' and 'non-profit'. A non-profit trip meant there was no money to be made from it. The standard rate of travel-expense remuneration was quite low—no more than 100 yuan a day for food, accommodation and travel included—and so anyone going on this kind of trip would actually end up out of pocket. 'Profitable travel' was a different story, an opportunity to cash in. Even by just casually putting out your hand you could net a few thousand yuan. Everyone wanted to go on this type of business trip, but no one wanted to go on the 'unprofitable' trips. This was one of the main reasons why Zhou Weidong and the others kissed my ass—I had the right to decide their business travel.

The sales fair was a supreme example of profitable travel. The company gave us a one per cent discretionary expense fund, which we could 'spend according to requirements.' 'Spend according to requirements' was a beautifully subtle phrase. Everyone understood this and secretly made money. Even Fatty Dong dropped his habitual fake-righteousness, crying and shouting that he was going to the Chongqing fair. Fuck, just for that tiny rake-off? I wasn't greedy; I'd settle for just thirty per cent of that one per cent. This meant that if 3 million yuan of goods were ordered, I would make 9000 yuan. It was simple to avoid any difficulties after the event: you just needed to take back a big bunch of hotel and dining receipts. The clients would help you arrange everything so there was no trouble back home.

My most recent trip to Chongqing arguably belonged to a third kind. It was hard to say whether it was profitable or unprofitable. When Liu Three went he'd lost over 1000 yuan and got a slapping. In my case, I spent loads on food, drink and Old Lai's Young Lover, but finally lined up a profit of 50,000. All the same, remembering this made me angry because that damned Old Lai had recently repaid the company 150,000 but still hadn't given me the 50,000 as promised.

As soon as the sales fair was over, I resolved that I would go to Chongqing and urge Old Lai to pay up. At the same time I'd get someone to file a suit against him. If he dared cheat me, I'd make him cough up the full 250,000.

I was in charge of the Dachuan, Nanchong, Neijiang and

Zigong regions. After returning from a circuit of my territory, I had more than 10,000 in my wallet. Zeng Jiang from Dachuan was a new client this year. He courteously sent me a big parcel with a packet of Zhonghua cigarettes, two bottles of five-grain spirit, and loads of lamp shadow beef. This time he'd made at least 150,000 yuan, and the bridge of his nose almost collapsed from smiling. I also felt pretty good by the time I got on the train home. Sat by the window, I struck up a conversation with two girls in the lower bunk. They were of the new generation. One was dressed in what looked like a net curtain and the other could have stepped out of the canvas of an old master. First I flattered them that they looked quite cute, and then praised their great bodies.

They laughed and one said, 'You're smart enough not to just say we're cute.'

After some careful questioning, I discovered they were fresh graduates of Chengdu University and were looking for jobs.

'Come to my company!' I said. 'I need two secretaries.'

They asked me what I did, and I said I was an independent director of the Pan-Pacific Sweaty Foot Group and CEO of the Chinese Smelly Tofu company.

They both laughed. 'No way. You're smelly enough, don't make us stink as well.'

The word 'make' aroused lecherous thoughts in me. The taller one wore a mini skirt, and sat cross-legged. Her black panties were just visible, which made my heart flutter.

Throughout this business trip I hadn't been with any women at all. The last night, in Dachuan, I lay in bed tossing and turning, unable to sleep. I switched through all the TV channels from beginning to end until my mind was full of commercials. Soft drinks that sounded like the urine of the gods. Some western medicine puffed up as a Japanese tonic pill. It could cure any disease you had, and just a sniff would prevent constipation. The funniest though were the commercials for sanitary napkins. You could move whichever way you wanted without any leakage, and the way they described them made them sound like a respirator. Just when I was feeling bored, the hotel sauna called to ask if I needed a massage. When I asked the price, they said it was 100 yuan plus a 300 yuan tip, which seemed reasonable. I asked them to send up some girls. The first girl had freckles, which was a turn-off, so I declined her services. The second was too skinny, which would definitely be uncomfortable, so I said no. The third was too old, the fourth too short, and the fifth had a cigarette burn on her arm. In the end I didn't want any of them. When I'd seen the lot, the female boss furiously cursed me on the phone.

'Asshole. If you've no money, then why don't you fuck yourself.'

She said she hoped that I'd wank myself to death. Not knowing whether to laugh or cry, I hung up the phone.

The problem wasn't really the girls, the problem was me. In the past few years I'd played around so much I'd gradually grown weary of copulation. Chen Chao said that

the Yellow Emperor had slept with a thousand women and
ended up a god. He complained that he'd almost caught
up with our ancestor, but instead had nearly got the pox.
When I thought about it, whoring was really very dull.
You spent 400 yuan just to do push-ups, and then when
it was over you parted company. You never got to know
the other person. It was a profitless business. I was becoming more and more afraid of the empty feeling that came
after ejaculation. Everyone had gone and there was just
me lying naked on the bed. Everything would collapse,
and the world that had lost its desire would gradually turn
grey. Where was my life? My ambitions? I had no enthusiasm for anything, and all this negativity flooded my mind.
A voice in my head constantly asked: Chen Zhong, is this
what you wanted?

It wasn't what I wanted. I wanted kisses, hugs, and
staring gently into each other's eyes. I even wanted lies
that would eventually be exposed, rather than just that
piston movement. I'd developed a dread of the night. The
slightest sound could wake me up. When I opened my
eyes in the darkness, everything I looked at seemed distorted. The lamplight was a dead man's eyes, the curtains
were a murderer's overcoat. Once I hung my leather belt
over the bed headboard. When I woke in the night it had
become a snake wriggling towards me. I was terrified. At
such times, I really did wish that a certain other person
was beside me, her hands on my chest, or lying in my
arms chatting away about something. Ordering me to get
her some tea. When it was dawn, she would kiss me and

tap my head. 'You pig, if you don't get up now you'll be late.'

I hadn't heard from Zhao Yue after that night at the Golden Bay. I'd assumed she would call and interrogate me, and had worked out responses to anything she might say. I might call her a cheap slag, or perhaps stupid for not realising I was setting her up. Maybe I wouldn't even answer the phone, just let her stew. Cry! Hate! Die! I would stand back smiling.

But she didn't call, and this gave me a sense of loss. It was as if I'd punched at thin air. The day she got married I'd planned to congratulate her, and again had my words all ready: 'The adulterers finally make it legal'. Then I'd spit loudly. When I called however, I found that Zhao Yue had gone so far as to change her mobile number.

That night when I woke up in Neijiang, my head hurt as if it was about to split open. But while my limbs felt weak, my mind couldn't have been more awake. When I thought about the twenty-eight years during which I'd squandered everything and struggled without ever catching hold of anything, I felt like shit. I guessed Zhao Yue and Yang Tao were probably in bed right now. I wondered whether she was giving him a blow job, gagging as her head moved backwards and forwards. The more I thought about it, the angrier I got. I kicked the quilt off the bed. Fuck! It's not over yet.

After sleeping the whole night on the train, my mouth

was sour. I had also woken with an erection and had to recite some of Chairman Mao's quotations before I dared get off the bed. This technique was learned from our department head who'd said famously: Politics results in impotence, while literature cures impotence.

So to be safe I recited two lines of poetry:

Pull up my pants and get off the bed
Anyone see my shoes?

The two girls rocked with laugher, saying, 'General Manager Stinky, we didn't expect you to be a poet!'

Ever since I'd told them my position, they'd addressed me as General Manager Stinky. I smiled invited them to eat lamp shadow beef with me. As I handed it round, I casually touched the taller girl. She blushed, but she didn't shrink away and I felt a jolt of happiness. The more I looked at her, the more beautiful she seemed and the more I felt that she was my type. I couldn't help laughing happily.

After we'd chatted for another thirty minutes, the train arrived in Chengdu. The sky was overcast and, as always, the north railway station was rowdy. The crowds at the exits were like ants after a flood, biting, ripping and pulling at each other to be first to crawl into this dangerous city. They would dig holes into every small alley and house, then creep in and bury themselves, never to emerge again.

I insisted on seeing the two girls home. They said there

was no need so I looked serious and warned them about the dangers of society. 'There are bad guys everywhere. The way you look will have a negative influence on society—everyone will stare at you. As a responsible citizen, how can I stand aside and do nothing while the crime rate soars?'

They both laughed. 'You're the one most like a bad guy,' one said, 'and you're warning us about others?'

Girls these days all loved a bad guy. As long as you had a smooth tongue and weren't easily daunted, you could have your way. You had to make sure you didn't talk yourself up too much though. People were contrary. The worse you said you were, the more they concentrated on your strong points.

Li Liang had never understood this. In the days before his diagnosis, there was a time when he wanted to study from me how to chat up girls. We went to most of the bars in Chengdu, and I always pulled a girl or several while he left empty-handed. Making a detailed analysis of our tactics, I discovered that the biggest difference was this: as soon as I opened my mouth I admitted I was a bad guy, while Li Liang always talked to girls about life, philosophy, and even communist morality. Oh, Li Liang!

Li Liang wasn't dead. He'd gone back to our old campus. He called one day, just as I was leaving Chengdu on a business trip. That movie *All about Ah-Long* was playing in the bus, the scene when Chow Yun-fat's character takes part in a motorbike contest and then has a crash causing a big pile-up. Chow Yun-fat thuds to the ground and rolls around, while Sylvia Chung and her son cry beside the track. You can see Chow's abnormally calm expression beneath his helmet as he staggers along and the sound-track tells of his distress: *That sad song returns to me in my dreams, telling of past times; those who turn around and look as if they don't care are lonely shadows left after crying eyes are dried by the wind.*

This hairy dude sitting beside me was choking up. My heart received a jolt when I heard Li Liang's voice and I said to him, 'Li Liang! Fuck, I thought you were dead.'

Li Liang laughed and said that in all these years, the times he remembered most fondly were our university days.

Before graduation, Li Liang had published an article in the literature society paper called 'My Homeland of Emotions'. I still could remember a few lines:

You can never find the books you want in the library. There's always the smell of sweaty feet in the dorm. There's a poster of film star Maggie Chung on Big Brother's wall, with her breasts circled: she is his ideal lover. On Chen Zhong's bookshelf there's a big knife. Maybe one day he'll kill someone. Bighead has a grotesque birthmark on his stomach, but he says people with this kind of birthmark will become big officials.

The overture of our youth was still reverberating but

I was in a different place now. No matter whether I suc-
ceeded or failed in the future, was happy or sad, in the
depths of my life there was a home I would never visit
again.

In some ways though, Li Liang had never grown up. He
was always thinking about the past. There was a fable that
summed him up. If you were given some grapes, would
you eat the big ones or the small ones first? I chose the big
ones, which meant I was a hopeful pessimist, overdraw-
ing on life. Although every grape I ate was the largest to
hand, the grapes themselves became smaller and smaller.
Bighead Wang chose small ones, which meant he was a
pessimistic optimist. Hope was always there but he could
never reach it. But Li Liang didn't eat grapes. He was a
grape collector.

Li Liang took masses of photographs on his nostalgia
tour of the university, many of them outside our dormitory building. I examined them one by one, and each
small scene reminded me of forgotten times: us sat outside the dormitory getting drunk; another time, when
we came back at midnight and made a human ladder
to climb the wall with moonlight on our backs. We took
pictures outside the building and sang 'The Internation-
ale' and Panther's 'No Place to Hide': *No place to hide
for shame, don't you feel lonely/ you have been rejected by
people before/ but you never have any feelings/ I have no
place to hide for shame.* Zhao Yue was in these memories
too. She would stand under the Chinese parasol tree with
her schoolbag and a lunch box, waiting for me to come

downstairs to eat, or to make-out in the woods.

Li Liang said that our dorm was still as dirty as ever. There were posters of naked women on the walls, smelly socks on the floor. The new generation of university students still debated our old topics: poetry, love, and their brilliant futures. In Big Brother's bed was a new generation Big Brother, and in my bed was a fat guy from Lanzhou. The woods that once witnessed my seductions had been levelled and there was a tennis court there now. Zhang Jie, who worked in the university office, had given birth to a 4-kilogram baby boy. The literature society newspaper had changed its name to *Sound of the Whirlpool*. Teacher Lin who taught poetry had died, and his wife had burnt all of his manuscripts. Among the remains was found a blackened piece of paper with one legible line: *The journey of life is long, there is no place to rest.*

Li Liang said, 'You have to admit, we've all degenerated.'

Li Liang the recovering addict looked sallow. His face was stubbly. His voice was hoarse and squeaky, as if a pig-gelder was gripping his crotch. I didn't agree with what he'd said. There was no degeneration. The stars were still the stars, the moon remained the moon. Walking in the river of life didn't make us taller or shorter. Our ups and downs happened on the surface of the water and were beyond our control. Twenty years ago I'd wanted to be a scientist, but the Chen Zhong of that time wasn't any nobler than the Chen Zhong of today. As I stepped out of the door, I thought that ambitions were like soap bubbles.

After they burst, their true nature was revealed. Li Liang's mistake was to mistake the bubbles for life itself.

CHAPTER THIRTY-ONE

Zeng Jiang from Dachuan County came to Chengdu on a business trip, and I told Fatty Dong I'd have to spend some time entertaining him. Honestly, I both envied and despised those agents who were on commission. I envied them because they earned more than me and the girls on their arms were more beautiful. But I couldn't stand how coarse and shallow they were, especially Old Lai. Quite apart from him spending all his money on whores, you never heard anything uplifting come out of his mouth. He called himself 'semen-sprinkling god' and boasted how he'd stuffed his gun into girls from thirty-one provinces, as well as conducting 'international trade' with Russia. The last time he came to Chengdu, we went to a nightclub. He grabbed a girl and bragged about his dimensions, using gestures to illustrate: 2 inches wide at the top, weight about

7 pounds, and more than 154 square centimetres. This
kind of talk was so unbelievably foul that my eyes nearly
fell out. The girls gagged as they fled the scene. Old Lai
was satisfied with himself, believing that his weapon was
supreme and he'd won the battle without even taking to
the battlefield.

Zeng Jiang, however, had the style of a scholar mer-
chant. He wore smart suits, expensive shoes and a
big smile. Any comparison was embarrassing but he
was the same age as me, twenty-eight. He was a graduate of
Shanghai Tongji University and able to talk intelligently on
any topic. I would often praise him, saying, 'You're a walking encyclopaedia'.

Once when we were walking around Wu Hou Temple,
a couple of foreigners asked us for directions. He chatted
with them in fluent English, while I stood at his side feeling
like a loser. I was rubbish at foreign languages, always con-
fusing singular and plural, unable to distinguish between
tenses. On one of the occasions when Old Lai conducted
'international trade', he asked me to do some international
pimping. He only knew one English phrase: fa-ke you',
which I'd taught him, for use when he was fleeing the
scene of battle. Anyway, that time in the Pushkin Hotel, my
mind was a blank as I found myself confronting a detachment of beautiful Russian girls. I decided to try flattery, but
I was careless with my verb and said, 'You is a beautiful girl.'
They laughed at me.

As we left Wu Hou Temple, I thought angrily that my
life had been wasted. I'd accomplished nothing, my wife

had left me, and I had debts. The knowledge I'd acquired at university had turned out to be useless. What could I do now?

Zeng Jiang didn't notice my dark expression and continued talking about how he wanted to go to the UK to study. I was silent. I felt as if I'd been robbed.

At that month's sales fair our Sichuan branch's achievements ranked first in the whole company. A triumphant Fatty Dong returned to Head Office to receive garlands. Before he went, he held a short meeting during which he boasted that he was a master strategist, surpassing Zhuge Liang[20] of the Three Kingdoms period. My lungs felt swollen as I listened to him; if he'd had to rely on his own pig brain there was no way we'd have got this result. Our success was down to two factors: good coordination on adverts and seizing our opportunity.

Lanfei company—our rivals—held their sales fair on 15 October, two days earlier than we'd expected. The instant I got hold of this inside information I applied to Head Office to bring our plans forward. I bullied the logistics centre to get the stock ready, then summoned Fatty Dong from his wife's side to convene an urgent meeting. We sat right through till three in the morning, until finally we'd decided a detailed plan. By that time this so-called master of strategy was only capable of nodding his head. He didn't even have a fart to offer.

That was the second day after Li Liang had gone missing. Leaving the office, I'd noticed the moon scattering

irregular beams in the alleys between the clusters of buildings. Apart from the occasional shooting star, the whole city
was still and silent. I'd slowly made my way back to my
deserted home thinking of Li Liang, my heart like a stretch
of empty desert—endless, solitary, not even a blade of grass
growing there.

On 24 October it was my twenty-ninth birthday. My
mother called me at work and told me to come home
for dinner. She said she'd cooked a lot of food and my
father had already poured the wine. I laughed soundlessly.
Although I didn't know why, I felt slightly pained.

That night, though, we had a happy meal together. My
mother's beef was hot enough to bring tears to our eyes,
but we wolfed it down. The old man challenged me. He
said that tonight he would drink me under the table. Heroically I managed two glasses to his every one, downing as
many as six doubles. Someone had got my father the wine
wholesale from Quanxing factory and it was powerful. I felt
warm from head to toe, my brain flooded with a drunk self-
satisfaction. Despite his crushing defeat my father bragged
that thirty years ago he'd been more than a match for two,
even three, rabbits. Everyone laughed loudly. My nephew
snorted until his mouth split, then spewed his dinner all
over himself.

Before my sister gave birth to her child, she and her husband used to argue fiercely. When my sister's husband first
started out, he was just a small-time hack but his ambition

was great. He wanted to be a famous journalist.[21] He went everywhere, day and night, with his concealed camera. His unit had a dormitory, but my sister said she'd rather die than let him live there — it was damp and depressing, only fit for storing radishes, she said. So we all spent two years squeezed together at our parents' place. My sister and her husband were in the room next door to me. Often in the middle of the night their iron-framed bed would shake and clank. One night it got so unbearable that I leapt up and banged the wall in protest, causing my 'famous journalist' brother-in-law to be red-faced for days. In 1994, though, their relationship reached crisis point — probably some kind of something-year itch. They'd argue eighty times a day, then my brother-in-law would storm out and my sister would weep silently. Around the time of the spring festival they had another big fight. My sister was pregnant by then, and was trembling all over with rage. She shook her fist at him, shouting, 'You're an immature git.' My brother-in-law leaned against the wall, not saying a word. I protested that my sister was being unreasonable, that nagging was wrong. My sister got so angry that she beat her swollen stomach. Full of indignation she shouted, 'Heavens, even you won't take my side. You don't know he has a lover?'

Now I realise how normal this kind of thing was. As I walked around Chengdu, there was no way to tell whether the men I saw were honest, the women faithful. Betrayal and self-indulgence were the characteristics of the age. It was just as Bighead Wang said: Everyone plays the field.

But back in 1994, the Chen Zhong who still had some illu-
sions about love was so angry that he almost smashed the
floorboards. He charged at his brother-in-law with a roar.
Looking back on it now, I see the whole thing as some
parable about human nature. My sister sobbed loudly, my
mother wept softly, and my brother-in-law ended up with
his arse on the floor, shaking and moaning, his head in his
hands.

It proved difficult for my sister to get past this affair.
For months she waged cold war against her husband.
Sometimes I wondered whether DuDu's poor health was
the result of all this. It was definitely a tough time for my
brother-in-law too, having to put up with my supercilious
looks and my father's and mother's cold faces. But he sin-
cerely repented and, after working on my sister's emotions,
finally won me over too. My sister moved in with him and
got her health back. She sold cars and enjoyed being a good
wife and mother.

My brother-in-law's career had gone well in recent
years. He'd broken several big stories, and had even been
to the Middle East once. In fact, it was said that he was
about to be promoted to deputy editor. My sister's face
was radiant these days. Every time she came round, out
poured a torrent of admiration for her husband's achievements. What was more, these days he never forgot to call
her and report his whereabouts. Each month he handed
over his salary right away to the head of household affairs;
my sister. She gave him an allowance according to his
needs. As she had a back problem, he taught himself how

to give a massage and every night put his hands and feet to good use on her back. He jokingly described this as 'legal wife-beating.'

After dinner I played Go with my father. My elder sister helped our mother put away the pots and plates, then left with her family. From the window, I watched them walk through the yard hand in hand beneath a blazing building of lights. My nephew bounced along at their side like a small dog. My brother-in-law said a few words to my sister, who made a fist and then rocked with laughter.

Suddenly I thought about my former home and our old street at night with its jewels of lamplight. Only a few months ago, Zhao Yue and I had walked along there together. My insides were gripped by a pain which didn't go away for ages. The old man stared at me for a while, then said in a casual voice, 'Still not guarding your corner. I've taken three of your pieces.'

That day I'd received three birthday calls: Li Liang, Zhou Yan, and the one I didn't expect, Ye Mei.

Zhou Yan was now assistant to the CEO at a special institute that researched how to feed pigs. This seemed rather a dubious position and I asked whether her boss had any other requirements. She laughed and told me to get lost.

'You think everyone is as lecherous as you,' she said.

Zhou Yan was a strange girl. She had to know what I wanted from her, and she was always smiling, but just when I thought I could advance a step towards my goal, she would back off. Once, during an agents' meeting in the Jinzhu Garden Holiday Village, we sang a few songs together: *When it's raining I kiss you, in spring I embrace you.* My head spun as I pictured 'embracing' Zhou Yan in many different positions. After the clients had gone back to their rooms, I suggested that we go for a walk. She squinted at me, then took a swing with her handbag, saying, 'You … give you a little smile and you get carried away.'

Then she went off to her room. I couldn't tell whether she was amused or genuinely annoyed, and my confidence deflated like a paper bag.

Ye Mei's call excited me and made me nervous. This time she wasn't her usual cold self, but said 'Happy Birthday' in a very gentle voice. It made my heart beat faster. Father was still hopelessly entangled in my stratagems. Slightly awkwardly, I chatted with Ye Mei. She said she'd opened a small bar on Bacon Road, called Tang Dynasty Windmill. As soon as I heard the name I knew it was Li Liang's idea. For some reason, that irritated me. When we were students, the band Tang Dynasty had just become hot, and Li Liang wrote a song which he called, 'Dreaming of Tang Dynasty'. A few lines became famous throughout the university:

Seeing you smile softly again
Seeing your long hair floating again
The Changan of a thousand years ago

I see you suddenly turn around
A deep feeling far away as the silk road.

Ye Mei's voice was husky with a heavy nasal twang. It
sounded as if she had a cold. I told her to be careful of
her health, and she said something appreciative then asked
me: 'Have you got time tonight? Come and hang out for a
while.' Her tone was that of a spoilt child.

My mother was happy because she thought I'd found a
new girlfriend. She upended the game board and told me
to hurry to make my date. The old man protested that my
mother had gone too far. With great difficulty he'd encir-
cled most of my players and was just about to move in for
the kill.

My mother made as if she was going to hit him. 'My son
hasn't got time to play with you,' she said. 'Didn't you hear
there's a girl looking for him?'

Still laughing I went downstairs. When I started the
car, its worn-out engine gasped for breath like an asth-
matic old man. I manoeuvred around the bike awning
and the small shop, and emerged to a street crowded with
people and cars. As I remembered that wild night of con-
fusion with Ye Mei, and the following seven months of
one thing after another, my head felt like it was stuffed
full of dog hair. A real mess of feelings in there: happiness,
regret, shame.

Driving past the hospital, my mind turned to Zhou
Weidong. During the sales fair I'd arranged for him to do
a circuit of Deyang, MianYang and Guangyang. The guy

didn't get a single night's rest. By the time the sales meetings were over, his 'gun' was worn out, swollen like a carrot and so painful he cried like a baby. I drove him to the hospital and he tossed and turned in agony the whole way. When we arrived, the doctor told him, 'We'll test your blood first. We've got to eliminate AIDS.'

Zhou Weidong almost shat himself. My heart jumped too. Later, I realised the doctor was deliberately trying to scare him. It was just gonorrhoea. He had to go in every day for two injections, each one costing 180 yuan. Zhou Weidong didn't have that much money himself so he'd borrowed 2000 from me.

I'd written the money off. A female pig would become Gong Li before Zhou Weidong ever paid anyone back. He wasn't cheap, but he was forgetful. When he had money, you borrowed from him and he forgot that too. Still, the thought of it was painful, because my salary was now just a few thousand a month. The way things were going I'd have to dip into my savings again.

I decided to call Old Lai. At the sales meeting he'd sold more than 2 million, and with all the add-ons, his gross profit wouldn't be less than 300,000. This time he wouldn't be able to get away with telling me how hard up he was.

Old Lai didn't answer for ages and I silently cursed generations of his ancestors. Finally he picked up the phone. He said he was talking business in the office with a colleague and asked me to call his landline in half an hour. I pulled the car over at the roadside and vowed to fight with

Old Lai to the end.

At that moment Ye Mei called again to ask where I was. After hesitating, I decided to be honest.

'I want to come, but I can't upset Li Liang.'

Ye Mei spluttered as if something she was drinking had irritated her throat. She said in a huff, 'Forget it,' and then slammed down the receiver.

Thinking of her post-coital body, I suspected that something was wrong with me.

Old Lai didn't beat around the bush. He said outright that he'd no plan to give me the 50,000. I kicked my cigarette stub in the air, breathed hoarsely for a moment, then said coldly, 'OK, then are you prepared to receive a legal summons? You still owe our company 280,000.'

Old Lai just laughed. I wanted to put my fist down the phone and smash his dog face.

'There's no way your company will bring a suit against me,' he said.

I blustered. 'Sue or not, it's not in our hands. You just wait and see.'

There was a background whispering noise, like papers being shuffled.

'You trying to scare me won't work,' Old Lai said. 'Boss Liu has already promised me they won't sue.'

I should have sensed from this something was up, but couldn't prevent myself saying furiously, 'Boss Liu is HR, he doesn't understand this kind of thing. When it comes to business matters, our CEO listens to me.'

Old Lai didn't reply immediately. The whispering sound

intensified. Then, after about a minute, he said, 'Boss Liu is right here next to me. Want to speak to him?'

CHAPTER THIRTY-TWO

When I arrived early at work, Old Yu was waiting in my office for his 170,000. At the end of last year I'd bought 260,000 yuan worth of car parts. I'd heard that the government was going to increase the price of small factory parts and I wanted to help the company cut its procurement costs. I never expected that a few months later the price rise still wouldn't have materialised. In fact, the more parts that were sold the cheaper they got. I worked out that if I got rid of them at the current price, I'd lose at least 30,000. When I talked to Old Yu about a settlement, however, he said he'd rather die than concede anything. I told the accountant to suspend payments. After six months had gone by, Old Yu got worried and called to threaten me. He said he was ready to take the case to court. I laughed so loudly the walls nearly caved in.

'You do that,' I said. 'Start your case. You'll definitely win.'

By the time the court reached a judgment, at least another two months would have passed. Old Yu would be sick of the whole thing. And even if the court decided against me, the worst that could happen was I'd have to return the parts. Would he really be willing to give up as much as 170,000 yuan?

After Old Yu had thought it through, he got very depressed. After that he visited me every day like a well-behaved grandson, lighting me cigarettes, being respectful. He was stuck to me like a plaster and I couldn't get rid of him.

When he saw me, Old Yu's face instantly became fawning. He lit me a cigarette, made tea, and chattered away endlessly. Apparently his family were having difficulties. His kid was about to start school, and his wife needed medical treatment. His eighty-year-old mother needed to be cremated.

Forcing a laugh, I said, 'This has nothing to do with me any more. You should look for Fatty Dong. I've been fired.'

Old Yu's mouth fell open, displaying a row of brown front teeth. He stared at me as if he'd seen a ghost.

The decision from Head Office had two main components. Firstly, fire Chen Zhong immediately, with Liu Three taking over the sales department. Secondly, stop all salary payments, living subsidies and expense reimbursements.

The remaining 260,900 yuan I owed had to be paid off within ten days, otherwise the police would be called in.

Before Fatty Dong had finished reading out the decision, my face went as white as paper and my stomach filled with foul gas. I was petrified.

Afterwards Fatty played Mr Nice Guy, patting my shoulder and saying, 'Chen Zhong, we are colleagues. I never hoped to see this day. You look after yourself.'

His smile infuriated me. I kicked over the chair with my foot, leapt and thrust my fist into his fat face. Fatty Dong slammed against the wall like a mountain of lard, making a sickening sound. Everyone jumped as if they'd had electric shocks. I threw open the door violently, my hair on end and my teeth clenched.

'Fuck you. Just you wait,' I yelled at Fatty Dong.

This catastrophe was one hundred per cent Dong's doing. After my telephone conversation with Boss Liu, my mind went through everything at lightning speed, trying to get it all straight. Now I knew why Fatty Dong had insisted on going to Chongqing during the sales fair. He'd gone to dig up the sales contract from two years ago. It was also obvious why Boss Liu had suddenly gone cool on me. I visualised how they'd plotted together, dug their hole and then stepped to one side waiting for me to fall in. Those dogs—fuck! At the same time I felt a confused hatred for myself. I absolutely should not have called Old Lai that time. If Boss Liu hadn't been there, I could have shamelessly insisted there was no evidence other than his word. Where were the written records? What could the company do? I'd never dreamed the company would go so far as to fire me. Now it didn't matter what I said—none of it was any use.

In my penultimate year of university, I'd nearly been thrown out because of the notorious porn film incident. That was the first serious crisis of my life. Afterwards, I told Li Liang that if I'd been expelled I'd have lain down on some icy railway track, just like our idol, Hai Zi.

In the early 1990s it was the craze for university students to run some kind of business. Everyone furiously debated whether those who sold tea or those who sold eggs would be most likely to make a fortune. It was as if we had been rudely woken by a stream of piss and thrown off Chinese students' historic burden of: '*standing upright for heaven, giving our life for the people, studying to achieve saintliness and win peace for all ages*'.

We lost our minds in the struggle to be first; lost our way because we were crazy for cash. At that time, anyone who couldn't say that they'd at least been a street vendor was embarrassed. At the height of the business craze, our canteen door was plastered with every kind of advertisement: for books, for family education; the words all gaudy and enticing. Outside our dormitory a forest of small stalls sprang up—noisy from day to night, and crazier and wilder than the vegetable market. Every individual was a trading company. Our dormitory door was knocked at eighty times a day by people selling shirts and socks, instant noodles and hot pickled mustard, combs, mirrors and make-up. Some even sold condoms. There were lots of dodgy stories about people getting rich overnight. It was said that a student at Normal University had made several million from trading steel, and drove a Lincoln to class every day. Another rumour had it that a girl from the politics department had invested a few thousand in stocks and in less than a year had turned a million.

I was no laggard in this matter of making a fortune. I started a beer room, and then rented a book store, then a pool hall. I had a small stand selling cheap clothes and books. Finally, in the second semester of my third year, I hit on the screening room idea.

At that time I had a famous catchphrase: Money is earned, not saved. Even though I had several businesses, I never had much cash. My profits all went on beer. The screening room was a good earner though, the best of all. The English department's Hu Jiangchao hired it for three months and even his piss turned to oil. Every day he ate all three meals outside campus. My requirements at that time weren't so great. I just wanted to be able to buy Zhao Yue some clothes once in a while, and treat friends to the occasional meal.

I was in the film business for nearly a whole semester, and made a stack of money, but finally lost it all.

At the start, trade wasn't that great. Each day there were only around fifty or sixty customers and the box office didn't come close to covering the rental fee. I went everywhere to get big films: *Gone with the Wind*, *Waterloo Bridge*, *Jurassic*

Park, Silence of the Lambs, and the Kung Fu films of Hong Kong star Chow Yun-fat. I pasted up enough posters to blot out the sun and cover the earth. Every Saturday I screened one session of classics, then all through the night showed TV programs popular from our youth. Suddenly the business took off. On the best day I sold more than 400 tickets. When you added sales of soda, melon, bread, cigarettes and so on, our profit was more than 1200. I soon felt sick from smiling.

The holidays began on 2 July. I'd planned to suspend my business and go with Zhao Yue to the north-east to enjoy a vacation. However, the PE department's Hao Feng came looking for me and handed me three porn movies: *Lady Chatterley's Lover, I'm Crazy For It* and *Sex and Zen.*

He pleaded with me for ages to put them on, saying that I could charge whatever price I liked. My resolve slowly weakened. I reflected that there hadn't been an inspection for ages, so it was unlikely anything would go wrong. Showing the films would also avert the possibility of any trouble from the jocks. However, I never expected the guy to immediately round up an audience of thirty or more guys. I got nervous and told him, 'Too many people, it's not safe. I can't do this.'

Hao Feng encouraged the jocks to join him in egging me on. They came out with a load of horse shit, saying I'd be a hero. After a while I couldn't resist any longer. Heroically I said, 'Let's do it. If the sky falls down I'll hold it up.'

Some poet once said that 'life is a river' and I understood. Beneath the smooth surface of the river there were dangerous undercurrents. A little carelessness could lead to the boat overturning.

If I hadn't been so impetuous that day, I'd never have been barred from getting an honours degree. And if I'd got my honours degree, I wouldn't have been rejected by the provincial Communist Party Committee propaganda department and forced to take a job at a car company. If I hadn't gone to the car company, I wouldn't be staggering along now like a stray dog in the polluted air by the West Station. My vision was blurred, my face twisted and my spirit depressed.

On that summer night seven years before in the screening room, porn goddesses Ye Zimei and Xu Jinjiang were having a big battle in a bathtub. More than thirty guys, saliva dribbling down their chins, watched as the girls stripped each other. With more than 200 yuan in my hands, I was laughing. Then, suddenly, the door was kicked in, the lights turned up. The security department's Boss Tang brutally ordered me to go with him. Behind him, several security guards scoured the room like nationalist bandits searching the mountains. The place was thrown into chaos. There was a clamour of running footsteps, of seats banging, of confused voices. Two guys tried to flee through the window, but were stopped by Old Tang's cry: 'Not one of you leave! Call their faculty heads to take charge of them!'

Then he grabbed me. 'You, come with me at once to the security office!'

I felt like the whole world had collapsed. Hao Feng tried to apologise, but I pushed him away and staggered with

Old Tang towards the security office. Once there I couldn't support myself any more, and had to lean against the wall, gasping for breath, my arms and legs turned to water.

I was prepared to die. I vowed tearfully to my faculty head that if the university expelled me, I'd jump from the sixteenth floor of the teaching building. This scared the old guy so much that his face turned white. He went to the student administration office and risked his position to say good things about me. Meanwhile, I got together all my profits from the past few months, about 10,000, and distributed them as bribes to the Dean's office and the student administration office. Finally I handed a fat red envelope to the deputy university head who was in charge of student affairs. At first he took the moral high ground, treating me like a crook, attacking my shamelessness in trying to buy personal favours. After I'd pleaded with him, and sworn to keep it a secret, he finally accepted, looking embarrassed. Still wearing his holier-than-thou holy face he told me, 'OK, you won't be expelled. Go back to your dorm.'

From then on, I was very clear about one thing: in this world there was no evil that couldn't be redeemed by money. There was no incorruptible virtue. Li Liang was very indignant and wrote a poem proclaiming:

Even if I can't ever be forgiven
I want to cry out loudly in hell
Saints … my sin
Originates from you gods.

Back then we were all quite innocent. No one questioned the cause of this disaster. It wasn't until three years later, when my old squeeze Black Peony got married, that I suddenly saw the light.

When I first started getting serious with Zhao Yue, I was still with Black Peony. My behaviour of having a foot in two boats made her angry and she often called me inhuman. She was one of those girls who is outwardly coarse but inwardly refined. When she took off her clothes, her body was very hairy. One night just before lights out, she called me downstairs and said fiercely, 'Do you want me or her?'

I prevaricated for ages before finally finding some courage. 'I have the stronger feeling for Zhao Yue,' I told her.

Black Peony made a massive fist. It seemed inevitable that she was going to hit me and I shut my eyes, preparing for her thunderbolt. Luckily for my face, nothing happened. When I opened my eyes again, I saw that she was going back upstairs, her shoulders rising and falling in the moonlight.

Anyway, her groom, a big manly Inner Mongolian guy from the PE department called Yao Zhiqiang, had been in the screening room that night. He was one of just two people who didn't get dragged off to the security office.

Plant melons and you get melons; plant beans and you get beans. A Buddhist monk said: Misfortune and disaster have no roots. Everything is brought on by yourself. The mountains before you were created by your eyes.

Standing in the middle of busy West Station, without a

job, a house or a wife, I thought: you, Chen Zhong, what have you made for yourself?

This Chengdu, as familiar as my own palm, was a place of danger, turbulence and uncertainty. There were always walls and buildings being demolished, holes being dug and roads being repaired. There were always vendors and hustlers who would grab your sleeve and harass you.

Carrying an insubstantial paper bag, I squeezed my way through the crowds. My soul felt as indistinct as the pattern on the sole of a well-worn shoe. In the bag were a few personal items from the office: a few books (sales and marketing), some certificates of achievement, plus photos I'd never dared to let Zhao Yue see—me and my breadstick lover, me and Zhou Yan, me with Miss Sichuan. I'd lived like a cicada that didn't know autumn was coming, spending my reserves of happiness as freely as possible. I'd made millions for the company over the past few years. All I had for myself was this small bag.

CHAPTER THIRTY-THREE

Actually, there was 58,000 in my account. Everything the old man owned wouldn't be worth more than that. My sister had some money until recently, but in August she'd bought an apartment. What she had left wasn't even enough for redecorating. Whenever I thought about money I had to fight an urge to bang my head against a brick wall. My insides were on fire. There was no taste to my food, and when I slept I had nightmares. My urine was as yellow as freshly squeezed orange juice. One morning when I woke up I discovered a big blister in my mouth. It burst while I was brushing my teeth, and it was so painful that I couldn't stop jumping around.

Head Office's lawyer had arrived in Chengdu. The day before he'd called me to say that Boss Liu's instructions were to spare no effort to get all the money back.

'Even if you run, your guarantor won't be able to run,' he told me.

I felt as if I'd ground my teeth down to the roots. I was desperate to reach a fist down the telephone and grab this rent boy by the throat. The guarantor he was referring to was none other than my dad. When I first joined the company, he'd signed a 'guarantor contract' vouching for me and guaranteeing to reimburse any economic losses I may cause the company.

My brother-in-law said this was punishing someone else for another's misdeeds. The old man still didn't know what had happened.

After I'd finished talking to the lawyer, I went home. As soon as I got in the door, I saw those two oldies squatting inside my room repairing my bed. My mother was still urging me to move home again.

'Look, you've lost weight. Of course, away from home you don't get enough hot food.'

Earlier, I'd decided to come clean with them. But faced with this scene, I just couldn't find the words. While we were eating, Dad asked me how things were going at work. Nearly dropping my chopsticks, somehow I managed to say, 'Fine, just fine.' Inside I was unbearably ashamed. I felt like leaping right out the window.

I discussed the situation with Zhou Weidong. He comforted me, and said that the company was making an empty show of strength.

'At most this is a civil court matter. They can't off-load any legal responsibility onto you. What the hell are you afraid of?'

But I was pessimistic because I'd seen how Bighead Wang handled such cases. The former boss of Yingdao company had been completely done over just because he'd imported a few cartons of fake cigarettes. He'd been fined and beaten, and had eventually lost his family fortune.

'Once you're in the detention centre, forget guilt or innocence,' Bighead Wang told me. 'There's just good luck or bad luck. There's never any chance to speak in your own defence.'

It was impossible to deny my debt. Anyway, if the company really wanted to finish me, they just had to give a few thousand to the cops. I wouldn't even know how I'd died.

There'd been no contact between Bighead and me since the Li Liang incident. I guessed he'd understood that unless he came up with an explanation then neither I nor Li Liang wanted his friendship. There was no need to spell it out.

Li Liang found it difficult to trust people, including me, his best friend. We'd known each other for ten years, but now I felt estranged I felt from him. This suggested that I'd never really entered his life, his heart.

Ever since he found out about the fling with Ye Mei, his attitude towards me had been weird. He was neither friendly nor completely aloof. Recently I'd got my mum to make a pot of Angelica Chicken, which I'd then taken to him in a heat-preserving container. When I said I wanted him to get better, he looked moved. But a few days later I went to his house again and found the container in a corner of the kitchen. It hadn't been opened. When I saw that the expression of my goodwill was growing green mould, I asked him why he hadn't eaten it, but as soon as the words were out of my mouth I regretted it. Li Liang's meaning was perfectly clear. He wasn't ready to accept any kindness from me. This attitude made me both indignant and sad.

I didn't know how he'd react if I asked to borrow money from him. For my part, I'd rather go to jail than be humiliated by Li Liang's refusal. At least that way I'd still be something of a man. I wouldn't have completely sold out our youthful principles.

In our second year at university, the literature society paper *Maybe* started up. It instantly made waves on our campus. Li Liang published an article in it in which he wrote: *We won't sink into degradation. We choose two kinds of death: brilliant or heroic.* This sentiment sparked an all-night debate, and was judged by Big Brother to be '7.8 fucking brilliant'. (7.8 was the scale of the 1976 Tangshan earthquake.)

My lack of funds had made me slightly unhinged.. When I went home, I noticed a black Honda parked outside my place. The back window wasn't fully closed, there was a two-inch gap. It was two in the morning. The street was quiet, deserted. I looked left and right, my heart nearly jumping out of my throat. In my paranoid state, my first thought was that someone was following me. Regaining some sense, I thought about stealing the car. In the space of a minute I must have asked myself at least twenty times:

should I or shouldn't I? Master Li of the repair factory had studied this kind of car and I'd learnt a few things from him. With a long bit of wire you could prise the door open. Selling it on would be a piece of cake. I just had to give it to Liang Dagang. It should fetch at least 80,000. As I was engaged in this mental struggle, I heard this old guy on night duty cough as he approached. At once I felt shaken by the reality of what I was doing. Sweat dripped down my forehead and my heart banged crazily. I'd fucking nearly become … a thief.

Actually I'd already considered various ways to get the money. Rob a bank, break into a gold shop. Highway robbery. Or sneak back to the company and start a fire, burn all the accounts: in court they wouldn't even be able to fart. At my most extreme I thought of buying a pig knife and killing Fatty Dong, Liu Three and Boss Liu, then fleeing to the end of the earth. When I was calmer though, I knew these methods were all useless. I knew myself: I'd never had the resolution needed to be a murderer. Could I really buy a knife and go to work on such a spectacular scale? No. On this point, Li Liang's appraisal of me had been correct. He'd said that if you loved money then money became your prison, and if you loved sex then your prison was sex.

'If you love yourself, then you are your own prison,' he finished.

The ten days were up quickly. At eight in the morning, the lawyer called to say he was generously giving me a four-hour extension.

'If you haven't returned the money by noon, prepare to receive a summons.'

Feigning confidence, I told him, 'I've got an interview this morning. If you want to go to the court, you can go now.'

On reflection I hadn't had enough fun, and so I added another sentence.

'You don't have to wait for me.'

And I slammed down the phone with no idea why I felt so wildly delighted.

There was no turning back now. As a last resort, I would suffer a tongue-lashing from the old man. If I could bear that then he would sort this out somehow. And if things really got bad I could obtain a false passport and flee to a new city, muddle along there for a while, then come back and live quietly. Anyway, I couldn't really care less. There was nothing I was reluctant to leave.

Strangely, the night before I'd dreamed of Zhao Yue. We were back in our university days, by the telephone kiosk outside the university gate.

'Here, I have a little money,' she said, concerned. 'Why don't you take it?'

These were the same words she'd said to me after the porn film episode had consumed all my savings. In my dream, however, I had this vague feeling that something was wrong. I smiled at her and said, 'I'm a manager now, I have money. Keep your money to buy clothes.'

Suddenly, the scene changed. We were on a balcony of

the Golden Bay Hotel. Zhao Yue was stark naked. She was weeping as she said to me, 'Chen Zhong, you've lost your conscience. You've lost your conscience.'

Then, like a crazy person, she pushed me. She caught me off balance so that I toppled off the balcony, still reprimanding her. 'You're always so damn moralistic. If we don't argue, your day isn't complete.'

That night the moonlight was like water, dripping coldly into people's eyes. A few late-to-bed sparrows were roused by the lunar brightness and flapped away. Inside a red apartment building in Chengdu's Xiyan district, an ugly guy suddenly kicked over his chair and grabbed at his own hair like he was crazy. Sky-blue moon-rays floated across his distorted face.

My interview was with a sports equipment company near the US consulate. They needed a sales director. Maybe because I hadn't slept well, I answered the boss's questions incoherently. It was quite embarrassing and I soon got the impression that he wasn't impressed with me. Finally, when I told him I wanted at least 5000 a month, his face clouded over. Ending our conversation, he chased me away.

After that disaster, I wandered around what was one of Chengdu's wealthiest neighbourhoods. This was where lucky thieves and successful bandits congregated. After losing their conscience and making their fortune by force, trickery, cheating and swindling, they changed their appearance. They bought flash cars, lived in fine houses and had beautiful women on their arms. There was a name for them: 'noble people'. Not far away, a bar had opened. It was said that it was frequented by rich women with fading looks and borning sex lives. They would go there to find youthful flesh. In 1999 I'd taken Zhao Yue there and encouraged her to choose one of the handsome guys sitting at the bar. Zhao Yue had laughed and complimented me: 'Isn't my husband enough for me? What do I need them for?'

Wandering aimlessly, I realised my temper had been bad for days. My mouth was foul enough to poison a fly, and so I bought some spearmint gum at a small roadside shop. Chewing slowly, preoccupied, I made my way towards the street corner. There was a Trust-Mart supermarket on this block and I casually glanced inside as I passed. Suddenly my jaw trembled and dropped. I froze to the spot, as if I was being electrocuted. Through a crowd of people I saw my lovely wife, Zhao Yue, carrying a diverse assortment of bags, her long hair swinging as she approached me with a smile.

CHAPTER THIRTY-FOUR

The day the cops came to our house, my mother nearly collapsed. She thought that I'd done something really bad. At that time I was naive; I'd never expected things to happen so quickly. The two cops were very polite. One was fat and had a thick Zigong accent. When he spoke, his tongue stuck out far enough to lick his nose. He asked whether it was convenient to talk at home. My mother's hands trembled as she looked at me dramatically. I put an arm around her shoulder.

'Don't be scared. It's company stuff,' I told her.

The two cops nodded and helped me in the lie. 'Relax, Aunty, it's nothing to do with him. It's someone else in trouble.'

My mother at once reverted to her usual chatty self, offering them tea, plying them with cigarettes. Grabbing a carton of Zhonghua from the carton on the table, I said to her, 'Don't bother yourself. We'll go outside to talk.'

When we were outside, I extended my hands and invited them to cuff me. They both laughed.

'Is this an unforced confession? Things aren't that serious. We just want to understand the situation.'

I played up to them. 'I've seen a lot of cop films — I thought that to speak to the police you had to wear handcuffs. I never knew they had officers as enlightened as you.'

This amused them and they laughed like drains. I led them into the teahouse opposite, thinking that Bighead had been right when he said that attitude made all the difference. You just needed to act innocent and the consequences would be less serious.

To deal with this mess it seemed I'd be forced to call on Bighead. When the young girl brought the tea, I made my excuses and went to the bathroom. I hesitated, but finally I bit my lip and dialled Bighead's mobile. This was the first time I'd contacted him since that episode with Li Liang.

There was a lot of noise in the background. Bighead said that he was eating lunch, and asked me what was up. Without beating around the bush, I explained and asked simply whether or not he could help. All the time I was thinking that if the son of a bitch even started to say no, I'd hang up at once. I'd rather die than beg for his help.

'Which precinct is it?' he asked, apparently smacking his lips with relish.

I told him the street name—I didn't know which precinct it belonged to.

Bighead muttered as if he was cursing someone, or had bitten his tongue. Then he told me, 'Stay with them and don't say anything. I'll be there in half an hour. You don't need to worry—I know a few people in the public security system.'

This gave me a warm feeling. After all, Bighead was a friend of more than ten years. We might have fallen out, but when it came down to it he'd still extend me a helping hand.

As I splashed water on my face I was surprised to notice in the mirror that I was still young. How had I got to where I was today? I lowered my head and sighed, guilty to remember how I'd kicked Bighead. In fact, thinking about the way I'd slandered him about Li Liang, I was so ashamed that I wanted to fall to my knees. If I survived this I would definitely get him that new notebook computer he wanted.

Unknowingly, I'd lost touch with the times. When I heard a pop song on the street, I'd listen for some time without having a clue who the artist was. The most 'in' things were a complete mystery to me; in fact, despite looking up the word in the paper, I still didn't know what this word 'in' meant. Anyway, it appeared that I was 'out'. Bighead and Li Liang were both netizens and often said that online life was tops. I mocked them for being boring, but I didn't even know how to use a word processor. Walking the streets, I'd see gangs of red- and green-haired punks strutting about and often thought, Aiya, I really seem to be old.

These last two years, I'd started to feel nervous about how I'd end up. Once I'd been the first to wear batwing-sleeved shirts, the first to have a pager and mobile phone. In thirty years time would I become like my parents, sat in life's corner shaking my head as I looked on? Would I withdraw to the shadow of my children, picking my feeble nose and remembering my irredeemably shameful youth?

The two police officers asked me about the background to the debt. Faithful to Bighead's instructions, I obfuscated, shutting up like an envelope in between complaining that capitalists were utterly scrupulous.

'They only allow us 100 yuan a day for business travel expenses,' I said. 'That's for food and accommodation as well. They won't even let us take the bus—they're afraid of making the company look bad. You think about it. How can they justify that?'

Then I let them know all I had done for the company. In 1999 I made them 120 million, in 2000 160 million. In 2001 more than 150 million just in the year until November.

After my rant, I remembered how in 1998, when I'd just become a manager, Old Lai of Chongqing had demanded the urgent delivery of 600,000 units of brake pads. There wasn't time to call in the warehouse staff, and so Liu Three,

Zhou Weidong and I had removed our jackets and carried the goods to the car, sweating profusely. In less than two hours we packed more than six hundred boxes. I was afraid the driver might rip us off and so I got inside the car, which was as hot as a bamboo steamer, and accompanied the goods. By the time we got to Chongqing my whole body was tingling and my arse was numb.

There was a scratching sound as the thinner cop wrote something in his notebook.

Unexpectedly he lifted his head and asked me, 'How do you write "exploit"?'

I couldn't look at him. Dipping my finger in some tea I wrote the character, thinking indignantly, fuck, how did I fall into the hands of people like you?

Bighead Wang arrived wearing a gleaming police badge. One of Cantopop star Yang Yuying's songs was playing as he strode in, upright and intimidating. There was no time for my introductions before he got to work.

'Your boss, your political instructor, I know them all,' he told the two cops. 'A couple of days ago I drank beer with your station head. He wanted a car and I said, If you can drink me under the table I'll give you one, otherwise forget about it.'

He had as much pomp as Pavarotti driving a horse and carriage. My ears rang as I listened to him. The two cops were a bit confused, but after they'd finished dribbling they thought to ask: 'Who are you?'

Bighead Wang lit a Zhonghua while I quickly introduced him.

'This is my Big Brother Officer Wang, head of procurement.'

Bighead Wang had actually been the second oldest in our dormitory, but he always disputed Big Brother's honoured position. He said there was a mistake on his ID card and he was really born in 1971, and so he was our dorm's real big brother. He and Big Brother had often fought bitterly over this. To be honest though, in our four years in that dormitory, Bighead had never done anything to make anyone take note of him. He'd never won a scholarship, never been a class monitor. He hadn't even chased many women. Apart from a game of mahjong once in a while, he'd never broken school regulations. So I'd always taken him as someone you could safely ignore. One time, when I had some cash from the film business, I invited my classmates drinking and forgot to call him. When I returned to the dorm I found him looking furious, and he wouldn't talk to me all night. Li Liang and I'd concluded that Bighead had an inferiority complex. Painstakingly I'd analysed this inferiority complex in all its dimensions: mediocre grades, mediocre knowledge, mediocre looks, mediocre family, and he can't find a girlfriend. How could he not feel inferior?

Looking back, though, it turned out I'd overrated myself. The Chen Zhong of 1992 could never have dreamed that he would fall short of Bighead Wang in every way—that one day Bighead would be his saviour.

The two cops seemed to have more questions. Bighead took over and basically didn't let me open my mouth.

He said to the thin guy, 'Write this down: one, the travel expenses are too low. He spent the money, but it was all for the company's benefit. Two, he still has some expense reports which he hasn't submitted.'

He looked at me and I lost no time in nodding.

'Right, right, our company's business involves lots of hidden expenses,' I said. 'We can't write receipts for them.'

This was actually the truth. Last year, faced with the threat of an industry-wide quality inspection, Fatty Dong and I had to be resourceful. Finally we managed to get to a department section chief and present him with a 5000 yuan red envelope. When the inspection came, he entered in his report that ours were products the consumer could trust.

The fat cop asked how much the hidden expenses were. Looking nervously at Bighead Wang, I was surprised to notice that he appeared serene. This gave me the confidence to say hesitantly, more than 200,000. The fat cop's face became stern, saying that I needed to think seriously: this could be considered as bribery. That is also a crime!

With a jolt of exhilaration, I understood Bighead Wang's plan. I sat up straight and answered boldly: 'You're dead right. At least 200,000 was given as bribes.'

After all, I knew this game. It was called, *When you meet trouble, first make the water boil*. This was something that our university's most respected teacher had taught us. Teacher Lin was a short, clever, well-dressed, smiling old don. Every year, whatever the season, he wore a tie, looking as if he might be called to the United Nations at any moment to make a presentation. He never wrote on the blackboard for fear that chalk dust might ruin his clothes. However, Teacher Lin had a brain with the capacity to astonish people. Astronomy, geography, religion, social and natural sciences—there was nothing he didn't know. At the end of each class, once he'd finished the official curriculum, he'd start on the unofficial. He'd talk about Lenin's syphilis, Zhuge Liang's piles, and the reasons for the destruction of Mayan civilisation. Listening to him, people would laugh non-stop.

During our graduation drinks party, we got Teacher Lin so drunk he couldn't find the toilet. It was the first time he'd ever taken off his tie, and he said drunkenly:

'Just a few more words, OK?' Everyone clapped. Teacher Lin stood swaying before us for ages. Finally he said, 'Today's lesson can be considered parting advice. In my life I've had a lot of sadness, so I hope that you lot won't be like me. These are the famous Four Life Warnings:

Don't give your heart to a prostitute.

Don't devote yourself to slogans.

If you meet a leader, you have to obey for a while.

If you meet trouble, first make the water boil.

Despite a PhD from a US university and many books to his name, Teacher Lin never married. Until the day he died he was always a deputy professor. Sometimes I thought he'd lived a depressing, miserable life. As to the last of the Four Life Warnings, today I finally understood its wisdom. It was impossible to prove innocence. If you're sprinkled with pollution, it's no good trying to prove that you're clean. The best thing is to sprinkle the sprinkler with dirty water.

Teacher Lin was dignified his whole life, but his death wasn't at all dignified. His heart disease flared up while on the toilet, and he collapsed naked and couldn't get up. This was July, and by the time he was discovered several days later, his body was smeared with excrement, and flies were eating the face that had always been smiling in life.

When the two cops left, I asked Bighead Wang what to do next. He said dourly: 'Aren't you afraid I'll take your money?'

I was embarrassed, and threw a fake punch.

'You still won't forget that? Wasn't I just standing up for a friend?'

Bighead Wang shoved me, nearly sending me flying.

'Don't pretend to be close with me. When you need me you call me Big Brother; when you don't, you say I'm inhuman. Is that the behaviour of a friend?'

I was stammering, I didn't know what to say. My face was as red as a squashed tomato and I felt angry and ashamed. I wanted to kick him down the stairs.

Bighead hadn't finished. After spouting froth for ages, he finally said, 'Fuck you. If it wasn't that I understood your dog temper, this time I definitely wouldn't help you.'

With difficulty, I managed a smile. Bighead started to get his things together, his back to me, still lecturing me like a section chief.

'You have to make this thing very complicated. It doesn't matter who asks you, you must insist that the money was paid as bribes. When they ask you who was bribed, you can just mention a few of the people you've bribed in the past.'

I went to interrupt, but he stopped me with a look.

'Relax, I'll suppress your statement. This thing definitely won't get out of hand.'

Finally I understood Bighead's strategy. He wanted to frighten the company into not proceeding with the charges.

As we were leaving, he said, 'We just need to convince them that if they still want to do business in Sichuan, they don't want to take the lids off those pots.'

CHAPTER THIRTY-FIVE

It was nearly Christmas. The Chengdu streets throbbed with excitement. Unscrupulous businessmen flew God's banner while thrusting evil money into their pockets. The shops were endlessly discounting, the restaurants endlessly delivering. Even the medicine shops offered special promotions. Buy two packs of condoms, get a free detox pack. Buy two bottles of Indian love oil, get one bottle of athlete's foot lotion. Completely insane. There were people everywhere. Chunxi Road was a sea of heads clustered together like mushrooms. Never mind what their family resources were, they were spending like crazy. The attitude wasn't like going to spend money, it was like going to steal money. Everyone was bristling with arrogance; even asking for directions risked starting a fight.

I went with my mother to take a look around and my

eyes nearly fell out of my head. My nostrils filled with the pungent smells of different meats and fish. Radish, flowered garlic, full-flavoured puffed rice. Smelly tofu. My head felt swollen like a big jug. In the Red Flag market we bought five kilos of preserved meat and two strings of sausages, then in the People's Market I got three shirts and six pairs of socks. Mother saw a gaudy traditional-style red jacket and urged me to try it on.

I bowed and said, 'Mother, your son is not a prostitute. What good is such magnificence on me?'

These last few days my mood had been much better. Last week Zhou Weidong called to give me some inside information. He said that Fatty Dong and that deadhead Liu Three had been cursing me terribly. I had him tell me exactly what they said, and it was nothing but 'mean', 'shameless', 'lowdown' that kind of thing, sprinkled with profanities. Their cursing lacked originality. Still, I bust a gut laughing.

I'd obediently followed Bighead Wang's strategy. The case had already moved from being one of misappropriation to one of bribery. The police had taken the bribery list I'd provided and gone to question Fatty Dong, Liu Three and the accountant. Fatty Dong was so shocked that he turned green. The police had also issued a formal request for the company to clarify the situation. The document included a few menacing sentences on product quality and tax issues. The words were understated but the implications deadly. I thought the big boss would piss himself on seeing them.

I was encouraged by this into thoughts of demanding my October salary, but Bighead shouted at me, and warned me against going too far. 'With this kind of thing you need to know to quit when ahead,' he told me. If I really drove them mad and dragged them right in it, not only would I be left unprotected but I'd also be in more trouble. I was chastened, and told him I understood. Looking at him with deep respect, I thought, this guy looks like a pig with a pig's brain. Where did he get so much knowledge?

A few days ago I'd had to go back to the company to get my social insurance book. The administration department was suddenly very quiet, like that old saying: people go, tea is cold. Apart from Zhou Weidong, everyone ignored me. All my formerly devoted subordinates had simultaneously become deaf and blind. None of them so much as glanced at me. Furious, I cursed them loudly.

Zhang Jiang, sitting near the door, took out some forms and looked them over without raising his head. I got mad and went over to his table and shouted, 'Zhang baby, you don't know me? Have you forgotten how you always used to ask me for things?'

When Zhang Jiang had first come to the company he'd got off to a bad start, and Liu Three had made a big noise about firing him. I had a quiet chat with him, and the guy opened up, begging me to give him another chance.

Now Zhang Jiang face's swelled up like he'd got uraemia. He couldn't say a word.

Zhou Weidong came and tugged my sleeve, saying,

'Brother Chen, forget it. Zhang baby also has his problems.'

I sneered, saying, 'Isn't this all for Fatty Dong? Do you think that if you ignore me, Fatty Dong will love you?'

At that moment Fatty Dong's door creaked open. Pretending not to notice, I drummed my fingers playfully on Zhang Jiang's head.

'I'll tell you what. The most sinister, most mean, most lowdown, most fucking shameless of all is that Dong!'

It was deliberate provocation. This time I had lost so badly that I just couldn't accept it. But Fatty Dong only dared to fuck with me in secret. I wished he would come out and really do battle! I thought that I knew him now. If you were polite to him, then sooner or later he would knife you in the back, but if you defied him then he was impotent.

I was about to leave when Fatty Dong roared loudly, 'Chen Zhong!'

His outburst was as tremulous as a held-back fart. Turning my head, I saw him making two fists. He stood in the doorway to his office, twitching convulsively.

I said smoothly, 'Boss Dong, what do you think? Do I understand you?'

Fatty Dong was crazy. He bore down on me fiercely, bellowing, 'You say that again! Shameless!'

The guy was massive; standing in front of me, he was like an iron pagoda. To be honest I was slightly afraid, but when I thought of what he'd done to me, the flames of fury burned in my chest again. My common sense evaporated as I glared at him as I wondered what I could say to really drive him mad. After no more than one-tenth of a second, it came to me.

Still laughing, I bowed apologetically, saying, 'Boss Dong, I did wrong by you. You are right, I am shameless.'

He was struck dumb.

'Although you only went to visit prostitutes,' I continued, I had the cheek to inform on you to the cops, and then told the reporters to come and cover it, to get you in the papers. I really treated you badly.'

I squeezed through the big door of the People's Shopping Centre and let out a long sigh of relief. Then I turned around and found that my mother was missing. I waited for ages but still couldn't see her, and so had to drag my aching feet and all our shopping to look for her. I couldn't leave without her—she had my wallet and mobile phone. Back and forth I went several times, but couldn't see her anywhere. By now I was furious. I'll really give her a piece of my mind this time, I thought. How could she just wander off like that? Didn't she care about losing her own children?

From the first floor to the fourth floor, from the fourth back to the first. My feet nearly dropped off, but still the old woman didn't appear. Finally I sat down on the ground, my body a wreck. Passers-by looked at me like I was an eccentric. I forced myself up again, thinking that I'd do one more circuit and then if I didn't see her I'd go home alone and leave her to worry.

The second-floor clothing department was swollen with

a buzzing and noisy crowd. I guessed that some brand had a special promotion on. Clutching my meat, I pushed my way through mumbling, 'Excuse me, excuse me. Be careful, oily clothes.'

The sea of people was parting when suddenly I heard a familiar voice saying tearfully, 'You ask him yourself. Basically, was it he who wronged me or me who wronged him!'

That day I'd seen a smiling Zhao Yue emerge from the Trust-Mart supermarket, I'd felt as though I'd been paralysed by the Monkey King. I couldn't move a step, my heart pumping with blood, nerves, excitement, and some strange residue of shame. I didn't have a thing in the world now, but there she was, as lovely as ever. It made me sad. Zhao Yue looked thinner, just as she was when we were first dating. As I stared dumbly at her, hate and love were mixed in my heart. I felt like lashing out at her, but I also wanted to embrace her. I wanted to rebuke her shamelessness and at the same time beg for her forgiveness. In the end I didn't say a word. Yang Tao was with her, and the two of them saw me but went right past without even blinking. Yang Tao tried to wind me up by hugging Zhao Yue tightly; my whole body went cold at the sight. I stood there numbly, my face muscles twitching so much they seemed to make a noise. As they passed, Zhao Yue, who had kept her head down, finally looked at me for half a second. What kind of look was that? I noticed that she was crying.

After that, I didn't hate her any more. Although I'd vowed not to believe in her tears any more, my vow to hate her was undone by her expression. The past was like a flood that couldn't be stopped. Every day of our seven years together, every trivial scene, was swept up by that tide. Finally, everything was washed out as blistering tears on my face.

> *Shed a tear, my darling*
> *Just one tear*
> *Can bring back to life*
> *In the deep level of hell*
> *Having suffered enough misery and death:*
> *Me.*
> —Li Liang, 'Heavenly Tidings'

Squeezing through the crowd, I finally found my mother.

'Don't interfere,' I told her. 'Come home with me!'

The old woman didn't want to leave. She'd waited a long time for this opportunity. There was no forgiveness. She started to sound off: 'Divorce, divorce! All ties severed. Why are you still living in his house?'

I shouted furiously, 'Ma!'

I couldn't take any more. I grabbed her hand and dragged her away, the crowd parting quickly around us. After we'd got clear, I glanced back and saw Zhao Yue sobbing on Yang Tao's shoulder. For that moment I finally believed: those tears were for me.

CHAPTER THIRTY-SIX

It was 24 December, a night of peace. Two thousand and one years before a great life had started in a stable in Palestine. From birth he was alone, suffering, before ascending to heaven amid the curses of the crowds. It was said that tonight he granted people blessings.

Actually, I knew that all days were the same.

Li Liang said once, apparently with some special meaning: 'Every year spring is green; every year the autumn wind comes. Life never changes. It's just that we get old without knowing it.'

I stared at the starless night outside. The Chengdu I knew was always overcast and polluted. Once in a while some sunlight broke through. Tomorrow, maybe?

A silent night in 1992. Li Liang arranged with Big Brother and me to go to church and see God. The word was that after the service there would be holy food. We waited until twelve when the hymns had finished, then the saints removed their white robes and revealed their real forms. Heaven's big gate clanked carelessly shut. The security guards at once started to push people away. The church was miles from the campus, so after we'd been expelled by God there was nowhere to go. We were forced to sit by the gate in front of the church, shooting the breeze, bragging, shivering and cursing that malignant God. When the sky was nearly light, Big Brother stood up and directed a long jet of piss towards the iron gate, saying nastily, 'Paying my respects to God! Amen!'

Li Liang and I rolled around laughing.

Christmas Eve, 1994. Zhao Yue and I were nested in a coffee shop beside the main campus gate, waiting for the glad tidings. The wind whistled outside. Inside, her face was flushed in the dim candlelight. Her eyes were bright as always, smiling at me.

At midnight, I kissed her, saying, 'Make a wish. This is the best time. God is watching.'

Zhao Yue muttered some incantations. After a full minute she opened her eyes and said with a grin, 'I know you want to ask me what I wished, but I won't tell you!'

I don't remember much about '95, '96, and '97. The tides of life rose and fell. In these years there were a few days that stood out, but many more were sunk in the depths of time, never to resurface. On those now forgotten Christmas nights, did I feel peaceful and happy?

When it comes to the past, we all get a bit sentimental. Li Liang said, 'Let's have a drink for Big Brother.'

I raised my glass silently.

'Drink up,' he said. 'Big Brother is watching us.'

Recently Li Liang had lost a fortune. In just half an hour before the stock market closed last Wednesday, he was down more than 700,000 yuan. When I heard this, I was shocked dumb. Finally I said: 'Futures are too risky. You'd be better to stop gambling. Let's go into business together.'

I'd been idle at home for more than a month, and was bored. If I could persuade Li Liang to open a medium-sized car repair place, with my industry knowledge and contacts, it would be sure to make money. I'd suggested this before, but he always laughed and said nothing. I guessed that was a refusal. These days Li Liang was increasingly hard to read. Everything he did had a hidden meaning. Shaking my head, I lifted up the glass and emptied the metallic-tasting Carlsberg in one go.

At this time of year it was considered unprincipled for companies to fire people. As a result, there were few opportunities to find work. I sent letters to more than ten companies. Some of them thought my salary require-ment was too high; some of them had no vacancies at the moment. I heaved sighs of despair, and lost a few kilos. My mother was still annoyed about my attitude that day at the shopping mall and wasn't talking to me. My situation really was pretty depressing.

I'd never liked the layout of the Glasshouse bar. The tables were too close together. If you farted, your neighbour would gag. But Li Liang liked this place, saying it was 'very Chengdu'. His implication was that only in a place like this could he feel truly comfortable. I thought it was more likely a question of habit. Wasn't life mostly this way? A minor change could make us all feel uncomfortable.

As the night drew on, crowds of beautiful women rushed past our table. Their eyes were painted blue and green, their hair was colourful too. Even in the depths of winter they weren't wearing many clothes. Their breasts were prominent their buttocks shapely. It was jaw-dropping..

I was enjoying the scenery when Li Liang quietly remarked that a few people were staring at him. When I saw them, I sensed trouble. I said to Li Liang, 'Maybe they fancy you.' My voice didn't falter, but the smile had frozen on my face. Not far away, Fatty Dong was glaring ferociously at me. His gaze had a green glint, like a wolf hanging about outside a village waiting for someone to attack.

Whenever I thought back to that confrontation at the office I couldn't help laughing. Fatty Dong had almost wept with rage. He'd made two fists just like a big orangutan assuming a posture. I wasn't sure whether he really intended to beat me or just wanted to intimidate me. I'd looked at him coldly and thought that if he so much as dared to move, I'd kick him in the balls and break his cock. During my days as a left forward for the university football

team, I'd had a famous mid-air swivel and shoot movement.
I knew there was no way the son of a bitch would be able to
take me. Fatty Dong shook his fists, his face terrifying, but
he didn't dare take a swing. He clenched his teeth and disappeared inside his office until I'd got my insurance book
and left. He didn't show his face again.

Seeing him here made me vaguely uneasy, although,
when I reflected on his usual behaviour, I relaxed. It
was well known that Fatty Dong never got into fights.
His mighty physique was wasted on him. When I'd first
joined the company, he used to brag about his so-called
morality, saying that such was his good nature that even
the shortest runt in his primary school class had dared to
bully him.

'I could lift him up with one hand,' he'd say, 'but he still
dared to jump up and hit my face! Fuck off! I was absolutely furious, but after thinking it through I decided not to
stoop to his level. Be a virtuous person.'

'Be a virtuous person' was one of Tiger Lei's lines from
the film *Legend of Fong Sai Yuk*. For ages after that I called
him Tiger Dong.

There were four or five people at his table. Among them
was a guy I knew called Liu who I'd met before, the one
who'd opened the wife-swapping club. We'd drunk together
once back in 1998. He had a reputation for having screwed
women from all the seven districts and twelve counties.
He had vividly described the characteristics of each: Qing
Yang's are flirtatious, Chenghua's depraved. Different districts for different occasions. If you want romance, go to

Jinjiang. In Jinniu, if you don't have any money, forget it.

As he'd talked my mouth watered and I'd smacked my lips. He encouraged Zhou Dajiang to go there; taking his wife too, of course.

I said to Li Liang, 'Relax. They don't want to fuck you. They're looking at me.'

As soon as I'd said it, I felt that because of his problem in the trouser department, I shouldn't crack that kind of joke with him. Li Liang didn't seem bothered though, saying with a smile: 'Well, aren't you going to go over and charm them?'

He was right. I steeled myself by downing a full glass of beer, then went straight over to Fatty Dong and his gang. A few people looked at me. I nodded at Liu and punched Fatty Dong's shoulder.

'Our destinies are linked, Boss Dong. Wherever I go I run into you. Come, have a drink with me!'

Fatty Dong raised his glass dourly and clinked it against mine, then gulped down slowly and deliberately. I was ready to go after that, but Liu grabbed my wrist.

'Why are you in such a hurry? You haven't drunk with me!'

At that moment I had a sudden flash of illumination, a sense that something was going on. But I looked at Liu's hearty face and ignored my intuition.

After downing his drink, he said with a menacing grin, 'I hear that you're doing some advertising for me, telling everyone that I opened a wife-swapping club?'

This was something that Fatty Dong had told me about originally. Liu's tone carried an implicit threat, but what could he do, I reasoned. He wasn't shy to promote his own joint. So what if I had been talking about it? After thinking it over, I turned to look at Fatty Dong. He was studying me with his mouth half open. His gaze was murderous, and his fake smile made me want to beat him up.

Something was definitely wrong. I hesitated, glass in hand, thinking that I shouldn't confess. I had a swig, rubbed my mouth and said with a laugh to Liu: 'I heard it all from Boss Dong. Why would I go everywhere doing adverts for you? Brother Liu, you're a clever guy, how can you believe such a thing?'

This arrow had three targets. It flattered him, got me off the hook, and fitted up Fatty Dong.

He laughed at my flattery, lifted his glass and drained it.

'I want to ask you about someone, a cop called Wang Lin,' he said. 'Do you know him?'

As soon as he mentioned Bighead, I felt relaxed. 'Know him? I know him too well actually, I said. I know all the moles on his arse.'

Liu smirked and his gang all smiled too. When I shot Fatty Dong a contemptuous look, I saw that his face was red and swollen. His jowls were quivering like a sow that's given birth to eighteen piglets. When we'd stopped laughing, he picked up his leather bag and stood up, telling Liu that he still had some business to take care of but we should stay and drink.

I said cheerfully: 'Boss Dong, is your wife throwing her weight around again? Does she need you at home to kneel before her?'

He didn't reply, just put his bag under his arm and went

to the elevator. But then he turned and looked at me with ashen eyes, like a dead fish.

'How do you know Bighead Wang?' I asked Liu.

He choked up, coughing and grinning. 'So his nickname's Bighead, the son of a bitch. No wonder he refused to tell me, no matter how often I asked.'

I'd given Bighead this nickname. In fact, in the last few years I had chosen a lot of names: 'Fucking Monk', 'Tiger Dong', 'Fatty Dong', 'Liu Deadskin', 'Zhou Trickery'. I'd given Zhao Yue loads of names too: 'Pisspot Master', 'Sister Dai Yu', 'Fat Sister', 'Tiger Sister', 'Street Cleaner' and 'Little Mouth'. The latter was to make her relaxed about blow jobs. Thinking of Zhao Yue I felt sad and poured myself another glass of beer. I closed my eyes and downed it, remembering that peaceful night when she'd told me: When I die, I want to die in front of you.

My hands and feet twitched slightly.

Fatty Dong had gone so there was no need for me to sit there any more. I finished what was left in my glass.

'I have a friend over there,' I said. 'You'll have to excuse me.'

'Why are you in such a hurry?' Liu said. 'I want to take you to my joint to have some fun.'

My eyes lit up. 'I can go even without a wife?'

He smiled. 'For other people that would be impossible, but you are Wang Lin's friend.'

This made me proud. I glowed in Bighead's radiant aura. Liu said to the guy at his side, 'Today's guests are Raise Flag, aren't they?'

When the guy nodded his head, my mouth started to water. Raise Flag were Chengdu's most famous tribe of beautiful women dancers. You could watch them forever. A few times I'd driven past the club and my eyes had bulged from their sockets. The car park was usually full of luxury cars, whereas mine was a battered old Santana. I didn't have the nerve to go inside so had to satisfy my craving by driving past.

Liu said, 'We're heading there when we've finished these drinks. If you want, we can go together.'

I hesitated. The guys with him stared at me. They were all repulsively ugly and didn't look like good guys. Ever since I was small, my dad had told me: 'Don't be afraid of fighting the wrong person; be afraid of making friends with the wrong person.'

In truth, I was a bit nervous about hanging out with them.

Beer really can do bad things to you. Although I had drunk just five bottles, I'd been to the toilet three times. In these last two years drink had ruined my health, and my kidneys were nearly done for. Thinking of the glory of my 'six-times-a-night' prime, I couldn't help feeling depressed at my decline.

Li Liang was still sat at our table, whistling like a child who can't find his mother. Light from the red and green lamps illuminated his face, making him look especially pale. My heart was filled with a strange pity. It was as if he'd just seen Jesus.

When Li Liang heard that we were going on some-where, he shook his head disgustedly.

'Sex maniac, you don't change,' he said. 'Sooner or later you'll die on a woman's stomach.'

I countered with a few lines of poetry: *If you die on a beautiful woman's body, to be a ghost is admirable. This is my wish.*

Li Liang gave me a disdainful look. 'Don't say I didn't warn you. Just by looking at those people you can tell they're thugs. It's better if you don't have anything to do with them.'

I laughed and didn't answer him, focusing my attention on the song and dance performance on the platform instead. A handsome guy was singing in a trance-like way: *At two in the morning, wake me/Tell me what you dreamed of/There is no news about people going to heaven/Or of what they leave behind.*

I felt confused by this sentiment. I said to Li Liang, 'Where is heaven? Life is basically just hell.'

He didn't respond. When I looked back, he'd gone. The disco lights were sparkling, the drums beating. The bar was a sea of shadows. To one side of the stage, where colours flew upwards from the edge of the red sea of people, my friend turned his head and gave me a stupefied look. He was like a corpse that had been dead some years.

CHAPTER THIRTY-SEVEN

A silent night. No moonlight.

A white van driving fast along Binjiang Road. The buildings along the road stood tall. Beyond them, the twinkling lights of the city. A pair of lovers embracing by the river, saying soft sweet things, laughing, sighing. A worn-out old guy wearing shabby clothes sat on a stone bench watching them from afar. His eyes appeared to shine with tears. What was he thinking right now?

My whole face was blood. My cheeks burned with pain. Fresh blood flowed from my nose and dripped onto my Gold Lion suit. My lips were grotesquely swollen, the flesh split. My mouth was full of stinking saliva and blood while every vibration of the van drilled into my aching body. A guy sat behind me, grabbing my hair. Liu's face was impassive. He cursed me unceasingly, giving the impression he wanted to rip me apart.

As soon as I got in the car, I'd realised something was wrong. The two guys squashed me into the middle so I couldn't move. Looking around, I decided the situation wasn't good. I said I needed to piss and got up, ready to leap out. Before I'd even got my head free, a guy in a black jacket threw a punch at me.

'Fuck you. Do you dare to run!'

He punched me until stars swam before my eyes. The bastard on my other side threw himself at me too, squeezing my throat. His strength was terrifying. For a while I couldn't breathe. My throat kept making a choking sound and I couldn't say a word. After what seemed like ten thousand years, the car finally started. He loosened his hand. I began to cough, struggling against them and asking 'Liu, Brother Liu, what does this mean?'

Liu looked at me sorrowfully, then slapped my face. My buzzing head smashed into the car door. I heard him say between his teeth, 'Screw you! That's what it means!'

Those giants beat and kicked me. Their fists and feet fell like heavy rain. Eventually I figured it out. Three months earlier Bighead Wang had taken a group of officers to close down Liu's club, and had put Liu in jail for several days. The guy looked tough from the outside, but apparently he was like a feeble grandson, unable to stand up for himself. Bighead had conducted his sting very thoroughly; from Liu's money belt alone he'd collected no less than 300,000. After getting out, the guy was furious, and vowed to get revenge on Bighead.

'I didn't know whether to laugh or cry.' I managed to say:

'This is a mistake. It has nothing to do with me.'

The thug's eyes widened and his knee stabbed into my neck. It felt like all my organs were done for. I dropped to my knees in the car but he hadn't finished. Grabbing me by my ear, he pulled me up towards his feet, stamped on me and cursed me.

'Fuck you! It was you who informed on me. Otherwise, how would they have found out!'

My stomach was smashed to a pulp. I tried to get up but couldn't stand. My head crashed on the rubber car mat, my swollen lips so torn and painful that I wept.

'Brother Liu, it really wasn't me. I never betrayed you!'

My head was kicked again before I'd finished speaking. As golden stars exploded before me, I heard him say, 'The cops have admitted it. Do you still dare to play dumb?'

What came next is a blur. I remember a small, dark alley where they dragged me like a dead dog. They surrounded me, continually punching and kicking me. Did I get on my knees and beg them to spare me? I don't remember.

Finally the punching and kicking stopped. I struggled to sit up, but had no strength. My head banged on the ground as I crawled along, until suddenly it exploded with pain again.

I heard a guy say, 'That's enough. Let's go.'

The night was as black as hell. For a long time I lay in that still, lonely place. I heard lots of different noises at the same time. The grass was long and there were flowers blooming. All things on earth were being born. The four seasons seamlessly merged. A few people passed by at a distance; some others whispered in corners. A tide of familiar faces washed over me and then retreated.

The tide swelled again. There was a sound of laughter, then crying. One voice from further and further away asked me: 'Are you OK, are you OK, are you OK?'

I was lying against a wall. Trembling. Cold. The cold filled me. It reached the pit of my stomach. Slowly the cold flowed into my arms and legs and bones. Every bone seemed broken. The blood on my face ran onto my chest and stomach and turned into ice. Once more I crawled agonisingly along the ground, my lips pressed against the soil of my beloved Chengdu. Far away I heard someone say: 'Rabbit, don't cry, be a good child, don't cry.'

My eyes were heavy. I could only keep them open with great effort. Blood was flowing into my eyes, but a few images became clear, like Zhao Yue's lovely nineteen-year-old face. A few things slowly became blurred, like the spring fog that covered Chengdu every year.

Shed a tear, my darling
Just one tear
Can bring back to life
In the deep level of hell
Having suffered enough misery and death:
Me.

Christmas bells sounded from afar. The whole city was rejoicing. In that dark, cold and dank alley, I lay silent on the ground. Fresh blood congealed around me, from which new grass would grow. I reached through the increasingly splendid Chengdu night and saw the golden brilliant God. Now he was high in the clouds, looking benevolently at the earth. It was said that on this night he granted people his blessing.

ENDNOTES

Chapter 1

1   The capital of Sichuan province in southwest China.

2   This joke is a play on the morphology of the character (寿) (shou) meaning 'longevity'. Chinese characters are built from different types of stroke. Chen Zhong is punning on the phallic shape of the 'dot' touched by Zhao Yue.

3   Yang Gui Fei (杨贵妃) (719—756) was a legendary beauty and concubine to emperor Xuanzong, of the Tang dynasty.

Chapter 2

4   Chen Zhong is making a mocking allusion to official political rhetoric and slogans.

Chapter 4

5 Du Fu (杜甫) (712—770) was a famous poet of the Tang
   Dynasty. In 759 he was dismissed from his official position
   in the capital and retired to Chengdu where he dedicated
   himself to poetry. The site of his former home is a popular
   leisure spot in Chengdu.

6 The largest carved stone Buddha in the world.

Chapter 7

7 Cao Cao (曹操) and Guan Yu (关羽) are leading characters from
   The Romance of the Three Kingdoms (三国演义) a fourteenth-
   century Chinese historical novel. The novel, based on the
   events of the Three Kingdoms period (220—280), is an epic
   tale of brotherhood and rivalry.

Chapter 8

8 Go, known in Chinese as weiqi (围棋), is a strategic board
   game that involves two players placing black and white stones
   on a line grid. The game originated in ancient China.

Chapter 10

9 Mount Tai (泰山) is one of China's Five Sacred Mountains
   and many emperors made pilgrimages there.

10 Bighead is punning on two homonyms, 'plate' (碗) and 'night'
   (晚), both of which share the pronunciation 'wan'. Bighead's
   question to Ye Mei contains the alternative meaning of 'how
   many times a night?'

Chapter 11

11 Karaoke clubs, where singing karaoke is not necessarily the
   main purpose.

Chapter 12

12 Mount Emei (峨嵋山), literally meaning 'delicate eyebrow mountain' is one of China's four sacred Buddhist mountains. It is located in Sichuan province.

13 Laozi (老子) is the ancient Chinese philosopher who is credited with creating Taoism.

Chapter 13

14 Beidaihe (北戴河) located some 280 kilometres east of Beijing, is China's most well-known seaside resort and popular with the Communist Party leaders.

Chapter 16

15 More word play. The girl's name is a homonym for (牛) meaning cow.

Chapter 18

16 Lin Dai Yu (林黛玉) is the doomed, beautiful and poetic heroine of the eighteenth-century novel *Dream of the Red Chamber* (红楼梦).

Chapter 22

17 A 'model soldier' of the 1960s.

Chapter 24

18 One of China's most famous film actresses, Gong Li (巩俐), first achieved stardom through her collaboration with Chinese director Zhang Yimou (张艺谋) on films such as *Raise the Red Lantern* (大红灯笼高高挂).

Chapter 26

19 Chen Zhong is parodying some famous lines by Xin Qiji (辛弃疾) (1140—1207), a poet during the Southern Song dynasty. The title of Xin Qiji's original poem is 'Ascending the Heart-Gladdening Pavilion at Nanjing'. (水龙吟·登建康赏心亭水龙吟·登建康赏心亭)

Chapter 31

20 One of the greatest strategists of the Three Kingdoms period of China and a leading character in the 'Romance of the Three Kingdoms' (三国演义).

21 The author is making a pun on the words 'journalist' (记) and 'prostitute' (妓), which sound the same in Chinese.

TRANSLATORS' ACKNOWLEDGEMENTS

This translation would not have been possible without the contribution of several people. Thanks to Jane Palfreyman and her team at Allen & Unwin, and to Nicola O'Shea, for their terrific editorial work. Thanks also to Murong's agents Benython Oldfield and Andrea Mingfai Chu for their support and belief in this project. Benython provided feedback on the translation and suggested key improvements. Special thanks must go to Claire Li for her valuable contribution to early drafts, and to the author for being an inspiring teacher and great host in Sanya. Finally this translation is dedicated to my parents, Chris and Carol Thomlinson.

Made in the USA
Lexington, KY
08 November 2011